OR WE'LL ALL HANG SEPARATELY

OR WE'LL ALL HANG
SEPARATELY

The Highlander Idea

~~~~~~

By Thomas Bledsoe

BEACON PRESS, *Boston*

Gatepost at Highlander Center.

The author gratefully acknowledges permission to quote from *American Folk-songs of Protest* by John Greenway, copyright 1953 by the University of Pennsylvania Press.

For Myles Horton
the most honest man I know

I wish to express my appreciation to the Louis M. Rabinowitz Foundation for a travel grant without which the basic research on this book would not have been possible; to Myles Horton, without whom the book itself would not have been possible; to Myles' wife, Aimee, Conrad Browne, Joyce Dukes, and other members of the Highlander staff for assistance throughout the project; to my wife, Boženka, not only for her work as secretary, typist, and research assistant, but for ideas and criticisms which proved of great value.

CONTENTS

"You, Horton," the judge said, rapping his gavel so sharply he woke the sleeping juryman in the back row, "what are you smiling at?"

"Didn't know I was, your honor," Myles Horton answered gravely, returning slowly to the drowsy microcosm of the Tennessee courtroom. "No disrespect intended."

"Then you're the only one in the courtroom didn't know," the judge snapped. "The court orders you to tell us what you were smiling at."

"Well, Judge," Horton said, in the mountain twang that more than fifty years of work and travel for human rights have not blurred, "I can't tell you what I don't know. But I do know what I was thinking, and I'd be right glad to tell you that."

"Just tell us, Mr. Horton, without the sarcasm."

"I was just thinking what a waste this trial is. I know what you're going to do just as well as you do. You're going to convict us on what the state calls evidence, confiscate our property, and put Highlander Folk School out of business. Then you'll all settle back and think you've got the job done. But Judge, you won't have done a thing. You'll only have

3

been wasting the taxpayers' time and money, along with a lot of ours. Highlander isn't just a school. It's an idea, and you can't put an idea out of business by confiscating property. We'll go right on regardless of what's happening in this courtroom, and five years from now Highlander will be doing more good, what you folks call bad, than it ever did before. We've been at it twenty-nine years, Judge, and they haven't licked us yet. You're not going to stop us now."

As usual, Myles Horton was right. The trial droned on, and in due course the Highlander Folk School of Monteagle, Tennessee, stood convicted on the grave charges of selling beer without a license, operating the school for private profit, and running an integrated private school. The facts that beer was not for public sale, that there had never been any profits from the school's operation, and that Highlander had been integrated from the day it opened in 1932 were clearly irrelevant. As was the fact that this was the first time in Tennessee history that a corporate charter had been revoked. The U.S. Supreme Court refused review because no federal question was involved after the Tennessee Supreme Court had dropped the charge of integration, and the great state of Tennessee revoked the school's charter and confiscated its property. After nearly thirty years of struggle and dedication, Highlander Folk School was finished. Justice had been done at last.

Yes, justice. Justice for those devout believers in poverty for the underprivileged, in free labor (English translation: no unions and low pay), and in segregation as an integral part of the American Dream. Justice — and victory — for those who for thirty years had hounded and attacked this bastion of democracy in the South with every weapon at their command: threats, intimidation, violence, innuendo, smears, charges of Communism and subversion, investiga-

4

Myles Horton in the courtroom at Altamont, demonstrating his opinion of the proceedings.

5

tions which produced no evidence but many headlines, and finally through legal action on trivial and unsubstantiated charges which never received a hearing in an unbiased court but nevertheless became the instrument of victory. Another victory was yet to come, but for today this was enough. Highlander Folk School was no more.

It was a day of rejoicing for those who would enforce their own prejudices on all who disagree. But for those for whom the American Dream meant freedom, equality, and the opportunity to live by their own beliefs and in their own way, it was a day of sadness and loss, however little many of them might then realize it. Highlander has always been a small institution, but its influence — and the significance we shall explore in this book — has been enormous. From its first days as an adult education center concerned with problems of poverty and depression in the South, Highlander has been training leaders who went on to train others to work for freedom, democracy, and opportunity in their local communities. Always the emphasis has been on people, on immediate problems and real situations; catchwords and phrases for their own sake have been in short supply. Freedom and democracy have related to very practical things, among others to the living example Highlander itself presented as a functioning integrated democracy.

And now it was gone. Highlander Folk School was finished, its charter revoked, its property confiscated, but the Highlander idea never even broke stride. Being practical idealists, Director Horton and his associates obtained a charter for an educational center to be located in Knoxville. This document called for a center which would " help adults assume responsibility and leadership and make the fullest use of opportunities in the democratic society." It also specified that this education should be available without discrimination as to color and creed. Myles Horton, who took out the new charter the day after the first one was revoked, specified that he would be doing the same things he'd been doing all along.

Grist for Highlander's mill, obviously, and confusion to its enemies. A house and an old manse were leased, and the work went on. Always, as one of its essential convictions, integration had been a fundamental part of Highlander's activities. In all its programs, in the early emphasis on poverty and in the long years of work in developing union leadership, emphasis was placed on the fact that racial prejudice was one of the great barriers to a free society, to a successful union, or to a community which would find means to solve its own social and economic problems. Example, not precept, was the primary means of education. At the school itself, any kind of discrimination was unthinkable, and as a result hundreds of Negro and white leaders left Highlander workshops, not only with their first understanding of the fact that they could work together, but with the beginnings of what were to become firm friendships. The theme was: it makes you no worse to be black or white, but it doesn't make you any better, either. What counts is the individual and what he can do.

For years before the Supreme Court's 1954 decision, Highlander workshops had been working on problems of desegregated schools and full citizenship. In March, 1960, immediately following the first wave of student sit-ins in the South, Myles Horton had remarked to a workshop: "I am convinced that these spontaneous student protests mark the beginning of a sustained effort which will lead to fuller participation by Negroes in all phases of economic and political life."

It was a sustained effort in which Highlander would inevitably play a leading role. Many of the original leaders of the student nonviolent movements had attended Highlander workshops; "We Shall Overcome," the rallying song for the freedom movement all over America, was a legacy from Highlander Folk School. Originally a Negro spiritual, then a Baptist hymn (food for thought there), it was taken over by tobacco workers on strike in the forties (more thought) who taught it to Highlanders working with them. Staff members wrote new words and a new arrangement and taught it to Highlander students, including those who would lead the 1960 sit-ins.

Its history since these demonstrations is legend. It is the only song in America which combines both the popularity of this week's Number One and the durability of the hits of earlier preelectronic days. From Selma, Alabama, to Berkeley, California, from New York City to New Orleans, young and old, black and white, will still, despite the enormous changes in the movement since the song first achieved popularity, spontaneously break into "We Shall Overcome" as the climactic song of a demonstration. On another level, it has become a theme song for a whole subculture of adolescents who are more or less aware of the freedom movement but have never joined up. If and when they do, "We Shall Overcome" will not be the least significant reason.

But few of those who sing it are aware of Highlander or their debt to it.

This is, obviously, a book about Highlander. It is also a book about the South. And it is, finally, a book about America and the possibility of achieving a genuinely pluralistic society here. It is, like Highlander itself, conceived out of a belief in human dignity and individual rights as simple realities, not just words to be used at political meetings and in

8

church. It is dedicated to the proposition that cultural and intellectual diversity are America's greatest heritage and her noblest potential. Conversely, it asserts that equality does not mean homogeneity, and that, while tolerance of difference is the *sine qua non* of freedom, we sacrifice a love for our own cultural heritage — whether White Anglo-Saxon Protestant (WASP) or Southern Negro or San Francisco Chinese — at our peril. Beyond a nuclear holocaust, facelessness, which comes in all colors, is America's greatest danger. And in facelessness all men are equal.

One of my heretical tenets is that the South, now the well of our despair over the senseless use of violence in the service of hate, is also, potentially, our greatest source of hope. Myles Horton is a symbol not only of the handful of Southerners who have had the courage to fight on, day by day, year by year, but also of thousands of others, not entirely quiescent or uncertain but having no viable out, who may offer something we cannot afford to neglect. The civil rights problem — or the future of the freedom movement — is not black or white, but black and white and a lot of other colors besides. Black power and white racism are, in my view and in Highlander's, two sides of the same coin, no matter how historically inevitable the former may be at this point in our history. In my boyhood days in Georgia, a poor white was no better than a " nigger " to those who held the purse strings. Their mutual hatred and contempt, along with their mutual hatred and respect for the ruling propertied whites, were symptoms of their struggle to get one-up at the bottom of the heap.

The poor whites won out: hence White Citizens Councils. From the days of the original Ku Klux Klan, polite Southern whites, those who stay home and gently deplore the violence, have had a genius for getting other people to

9

do their dirty work (a legacy, perhaps, from the slave system) and it cost nothing to offer mutual whiteness — and superiority — as a fee. And that's about all the fee usually amounted to.

The result, obviously, was more violence. And the solution, equally obviously, is the one Myles Horton, a WASP himself, and Highlander have practiced for more than thirty years. The problem is to eliminate the bottom. So what do you do? People have to meet together, consider their problems together, and take it from there. To do this, they must speak each other's language. And here is where hope may yet develop from the Southern white and Negro, a hope which is, among many other things, what Highlander has always been about. Negroes and whites have spent almost thirty-five years here talking *together*.

But there's another aspect. Highlander has always taken things one at a time, concentrating on immediate problems. This means establishing both an order of priorities and a framework within which this order makes sense. It's what, during my term of indenture in the Navy, they used to call the difference between tactics and strategy. Tactics is what you do today to meet the immediate problem. Strategy is the overall design into which tactics must be fitted. Strategy is what determines whether today's tactic is to fight or to retreat and fight tomorrow. The idea is that strategy is what ensures victory, and that tactics which are aimed only at survival and ignore long-range strategy are likely to result in defeat.

Well, organized murder has its lessons for the organized fight for peace. Hence the strategy of the freedom movement, the rationale for nonviolent resistance, in which strategy and tactics exist as surely as in a war where violence is the order of the day. The strategy of peaceful but unrelenting pressure to achieve human rights defines the overall method. But when a sitdown is to be staged, where pressures are to be exerted, whether demonstrations are to be continuous or temporarily relaxed — these are matters of tactics, and they must be integrated into the grand design. Though the weapons have been defined by strategy as nonviolent, they must nevertheless be applied in a systematic fashion if they are to be effective against an organized violent resistance.

If one of Highlander's functions has been to train leaders who can be aware of these basic priorities, both in the early days of the Southern labor movement and in the present of the freedom movement, it has also had to establish priorities for itself in other equally basic matters. When I first knew of Highlander, back in Kentucky in the thirties, it was as a labor school and an institution which was concerned about, and doing something about, the problems of Appalachia which Margaret Bourke-White and Elia Kazan were recording in still and moving pictures. Those who encounter it today generally regard it as a civil rights hostel totally committed to the Negro cause.

Both views are right, and both are wrong. Highlander is committed to all these causes, and to many more, but *exclusively* to none. Its full commitment is to a larger endeavor, the achievement of an equalitarian, culturally diverse but harmonious South which can serve as a model for a pluralistic America. In recent years, from a tactical point of view, the problems of the Negro have been overwhelmingly predominant; they demanded, and got *almost* exclusive attention. The Negro is on the march, thank God, and Highlander and this book march with him, brothers in the

11

necessary thrust toward that improbable goal, universal brotherhood. Now the emphasis is on the poor particularly the Appalachian poor, but the problem remains the same.

There are, of course, other strategies, other tactics. Since 1967 the advocates of Black Power, a concept in which universal brotherhood is definitely *not* included, have come to play an increasingly important role in the movement. I have already suggested that both white racism and black racism are incompatible with the Highlander idea, and in the last chapter of this book I will explore this question in some detail. Throughout, however, our focus is on Highlander's commitment to democracy in action, a method in which color and creed are irrelevant and of which brotherhood is very much a part.

The fact is that brotherhood is both simple and complicated. It means love and consanguinity, which latter term anyone should recognize as an attribute of all known members of the human race. It also means, in moments of crisis, forgetting small differences on behalf of those larger unities. When Martin Luther King, kneeling in the rain in Selma, offered prayers for Sheriff Clark during his siege of chest pains and meant them, he had truth. Those kids, white and black, who snickered at the old man's foolishness while they went through the motions, might better have been somewhere else putting in their time getting ahead. There'll always be another cause handy. Or a war, if that kind of battle is what you prefer.

All of which relates to the Appalachian whites I earlier referred to, in a nomenclature familiar to all Southerners, black or white, as poor white. Poor white trash, respectable Negroes used to call them in their mutual and self-defeating warfare. They too, even those who have taken the opiate of White Citizens Councils, that institutionalization of their ancestral hate, are part of the brotherhood whose hope I have posited, and whose achievement is Highlander's goal. That's what the Reverend King meant in his prayers for Sheriff Clark, a qualified member of the hate society. It's what you have to mean too, if you dig the idea. You can't preach non-violence without meaning it. Not, that is, and stay on board.

White hoodlums in Selma, roughing up nonviolent demonstrators, aren't any better than Negro hoodlums in New York, roughing up white subway travelers. But they aren't any worse, either. Both may be a little better, or a little worse, depending on the way you look at it, than the respectable community, white and black, which stays home, clucks its tongue, and does nothing except take a little profit now and then when it's easy and safe. Or the intellectual community which comments wisely and stays aloof. Or the ecumenical religious groups which, to their credit, descended like flies on Selma but, to their discredit, preach, back at the ranch, far too few sermons against American murder in Vietnam.

That's our world and if, like Highlander, you really mean business, you have to accept it all and go to work. You concentrate where there is the most hope and where you think you can do the most good. You design tactics aimed to fit your strategy for an equalitarian, culturally diverse but harmonious South, and keep working. And if you're lucky, and if you're Highlander, you get results that give the rest of us hope.

On these results, and on the assumptions I have been at some pains to spell out, this book is based. The story that follows shows both in action. And in hope.

Just one more thing. That final victory over Highlander Folk School, in case you've been curious, followed the usual pattern. Some months after the trial, when the property had

Myles and Aimee Horton at the ruins of the main house at High-lander Center. PHOTO BY MARION PALFI.

already been confiscated by the State of Tennessee, persons unknown, to use the standard terminology, burned the main building and a couple of smaller ones to the ground. All trace of Highlander's existence was forever eradicated.

Except, of course, in the hearts of men. And in the continuing struggle for human rights in which Highlander Center plays an increasingly important role. Myles Horton underestimated those next five years. In a three-year period, from 1961 to 1964, the attendance at Highlander Workshops increased by more than 400 percent.

Maybe they should have left that little old school in Monteagle alone.

CHAPTER ONE

Beginnings

It was some time after these reflections that I set out to visit Highlander Center in Knoxville. We were living in Hollywood, California, and in 1966 took the Southern route across the country. An apt route too, for an old Georgia boy, with a Bledsoe, Texas, just to the north and a Bledsoe County next door to Grundy County in Tennessee. Grundy County was a memento of Highlander Folk School, which had been born, banned, and burned there, and Knoxville, not Heaven, was our destination.

It was good to be back in the South where the air smelled like home. Even in the coldest weather in sixty-one years — it was nine below with nine inches of snow in Knoxville — I felt the warmth of the country I was born and bred in, of the easy living even the little old ladies in Hollywood can't imitate. I was home.

Almost.

There was just one thing that didn't smell right.

The hate.

I felt it first in Alabama. Texas was Texas, Mexico was Mexico, and New Orleans was New Orleans, with Gallatoire's, the Old Absinthe House, and Lafitte's Blacksmith's

Shop rendering to the inner man that which is the inner man's, but Alabama was different. In Eutaw, the town was closed down; only in the Negro section were there people on the street. In Knoxville — Alabama — where I stopped at a trucker's restaurant to call Highlander, two rednecks came out and glared at our California license. In Birmingham, at our friendly Holiday Inn, an ex-football player going rapidly to fat lauded Bear Bryant in the bar (Maybe Bear ain't the greatest man in the world, but I never met a greater one), cussed niggers, and rendered a hysterical laugh that began with a wheeze and ended with a whistle. His life had been consummated in the segregated backfield at Alabama ten years before.

Of course it wasn't just Alabama. This was where we hit the places it showed. In Bogalusa we'd have seen it too. Even in New Orleans, when I was taking a shortcut to avoid a traffic jam at the drawbridge, I was reminded that they still don't give Negroes decent streets. On Florida Avenue the pavement goes to hell when you hit the shacks; in the Vieux Carré, where the tourists and the strippers hang out, the streets are as smooth as heaven. And in Knoxville, the pillars outside the Center were smeared with red paint, and every morning at five o'clock we got an anonymous sound-less phone call. No message, just heavy breathing. In the town where Myles Horton is the most celebrated and most hated resident.

The Center is not an impressive looking institution. A once-imposing old house whose grounds rolled down to the river, it now fronts on the Tennessee Marble Company (a subsidiary of the Georgia Marble Company) and features an open shack which houses a pickup truck with a loose rod and an office in back where Conrad Browne conducts the business of the Center weekdays and Sundays. An ordained

Aimee and Myles Horton; Ora and Conrad Browne (left to right).
PHOTO BY THORSTEN HORTON.

Baptist minister who had the sense never to preach, only to act, Browne is now a reformed Unitarian and Myles Horton's good right hand.

It's a far cry from the old Folk School, with its big house, library, and community center, and two hundred acres of ground where whites and negroes could just wander and be people. That library, a glass-enclosed structure designed by Carl Koch, was the site of an alleged piece of integrated sexual intercourse sworn to by two notorious liars before the jury at Altamont. Apparently it never occurred to the Judge, now a Justice of the Tennessee Supreme Court, or the Attorney General, now the Judge, or the Jury, since returned to their duties as underpaid pillars of the community, that anybody interested in this kind of illicit activity would have chosen a more secluded spot. What with that two hundred acres and all.

But that's the kind of trial it was. And it closed down Highlander Folk School, confiscated and padlocked it, as the Governor of Georgia and the Attorney General of Arkansas and emissaries of the Sovereign State of Tennessee, if you're interested in States Rights, had demanded. But it didn't stop a thing. Highlander was an idea, and is.

It began where all important things start, between one man's ears. On Christmas night, 1931, in Copenhagen, Denmark, Myles Horton, a Tennessee boy who had served time at Cumberland College, Union Theological Seminary, and the University of Chicago before going to Denmark to learn about their Folk Schools, wrote this:

I can't sleep but there are dreams — a school where young men and women can come for a minimum of three months and be inspired by personalities expressing themselves through teaching (history, literature), song and music, arts, weaving, etc., and by life lived together. These people should be from the South if

19

possible. Negroes should be among the students. Some students should be from mountain schools, others from factories.

Such a school should be a stopping place for traveling liberals and a meeting place for southern radicals.

In the years to come the whole mountain side should be covered with visitors who come from all around to have singing or to hear a speaker with a message.

My idea of a good joke is to help make the mountaineer, who will be counted on by the industrialists as a potential low wage worker, dangerously individualistic and a threat to the capitalists instead of to organized labor.

"When all the faculties are wide-awake in pursuit of a single object, or fixed in the spasm of an absorbing emotion, they are ofttimes clairvoyant in a marvelous degree in respect to many collateral things, as Wordsworth has so forcibly illustrated in his sonnet on the Boy of Windermere, and as Hawthorne has developed with such metaphysical accuracy in the chapter of his wondrous story where Hester walks forth to meet her punishment." (from "My Hunt after 'The Captain'" by Oliver Wendell Holmes)

A school where young men, living in close personal contact with teachers, will learn how to take their place intelligently in the changing world which at present presents so many baffling problems to them. In a few months, free from credits and examinations, utilizing only such methods as individual requirements call for, possible because of the smallness of the group and opportunity for personal contacts made easy by students and teachers living, working, and studying together, it is hoped that by a stimulating presentation of material and study of actual situations that the students will be able to make decisions for themselves and act on the basis of an enlightened judgment.

In a period of five months an effort will be made to stimulate the students' interest and make possible for them a definite direction through a realistic presentation of subject matter directly related or relatable to the situation in which they must take their place. At the same time, however, an effort will be made to so relate the present situation to the world today that they will have a perspective and a basis for judgment on which they can act.

The approach used will possibly include few of the usual

education techniques but will endeavor to broaden the pupils' outlook and help them acquire definite information by observing, taking part in and analyzing situations of interest, by use of discussions, personal contacts, radio programs, etc.

A meeting place for Southern radicals. That's what Highlander has always been and, bless Myles, still is. Radical is a nasty word nowadays, but it, not television or the electric refrigerator, is the American Dream. America was a radical experiment, and the Founding Fathers, respectable and well-to-do as they were, knew it. If most Americans have forgotten it, it's up to people like us to remember it. You don't impose democracy. You let it happen. On its own.

Next day Myles wrote more:

I propose to help people face the world in which they live as intelligently as possible. An intelligent purpose based on moral values gives meaning to life and makes life worth living.

Students: An effort will be made to stimulate the adult to make decisions for himself and act on the basis of intelligent judgment.

Location: The school should be located at a place where there is opportunity for being alone. "Solitude," says Emerson, "takes off the pressure of present importunities, that more catholic and human relations may appear."

Life: Life is to be lived abundantly and daringly. Life is too spiritual to be dragged down by the material but too respectful of the material to separate it from the spiritual. Only by unifying the realities of life can dignity and the worth of a human being be realized.

I found there was a way to expand my world, and I insist on the right of others to live that kind of life, too. To limit the development of my own personality or the personality of anyone else is immoral.

Teaching: There is something creative about teaching. When we stop learning, helping others to learn is impossible. We might be able to pass on facts and predigested ideas but could hardly stimulate learning.

What I teach must be a part of me if it is to become a part of another human being. What I am and what I believe in and am searching for means more than anything I might say as a teacher.

It seems that the first folk schools were used by the three leaders in the movement as an excuse for having people around while they talked about ideas most dear to them. The methods they used were those best suited to their own personalities.

One talked about the Bible and religion, another about Danish history, another about the Danish peasants and their struggles. After all, about all teachers need is a kind of framework which enables them to stimulate other people along lines that seem worthwhile.

At this point Myles had nothing, just the idea that has made Highlander important. But within a year the school was an actuality. Ponder this improbability. It's the American Dream most Americans have reneged on. To dream takes guts, purpose, and intelligence. You don't discover electricity just by flying a kite.

So Myles Horton went back to America. He got his first contribution from Sherwood Eddy, a busy man of means like the Founding Fathers, whom Reinhold Niebuhr had recommended. Back in the Cumberland country he met Dr. Lillian Johnson, an extraordinary woman, as conservative as George Washington and as radical, who loaned and then deeded the property that became Highlander Folk School.

I'm going to quote Myles a lot in this first chapter partly because he has written so little. What I'm saying is not a paradox. Like Conrad Browne, he has had the sense to *be*. But what he has written is of immense consequence to this story. Highlander is not and has never been a one-man operation, but one man, Myles Horton, has set the tone of it.

An interview in 1959 makes this clear:

Highlander began in the fall of 1932. November.

How old were you then?

I was born in 1905. I was 28.

By that time you were through school?

Yes. I had graduated from high school and from Cumberland University, Lebanon, Tennessee. I was 23 in 1928. I worked a year as student YMCA secretary. Then I went to Union Theological Seminary for a year. And then I went to University of Chicago for a year. Then I spent months in Denmark.

Your trip to Denmark was motivated by what?

Well, before while in college at Cumberland University, I worked in the mountains for the Presbyterian Church, working with vacation Bible Schools and the educational program in their Sunday Schools. I found by experimenting that if you brought adults together for a free discussion of problems that concerned them without any effort to indoctrinate them or to limit their scope of inquiry, that there was a vitality there that I hadn't seen in organized programs. I discovered that almost accidentally and then I experimented by getting a group together at a little place called Ozone. This is between Crossville and Rockwood on the mountain. There is a little church out from Ozone. I was supposed to do a vacation Bible School for the Presbyterian Church. I had three assistants working with me. I turned the young people's part of the program over to them and I invited the older people to come in for discussions of whatever they wanted to discuss. They came in by the score. They walked ten or twelve miles.

Would you say this was the nucleus of Highlander?

That's where I got my idea. Right there!

I remember they wanted to know about farm problems. They wanted to know about getting jobs in textile mills. They wanted to know about testing wells for typhoid. We discussed these things. To my amazement my inability to answer the questions didn't bother them. I was afraid they would ask for answers to their questions. I was afraid. I knew I didn't know the answers to a lot of their questions. I gambled on being able to handle the situation some way. And I found that just by discussing these things and saying we'll get a county agent, we'll get a health officer, we'll get somebody else later on . . . that they . . . that I could be their educational leader without knowing the answers. That was probably the biggest discovery I ever made. You don't have to know the answers. You raise the questions . . . sharpen the questions . . . get people to discussing them. And we found that in that group of mountain people a lot of answers were available if they pooled their knowledge.

You are saying, then, that people can always find the answers themselves?

If you can get them into a free discussion and get them to talk as equals. That's the key to the thing. There's not much, basically . . . I learned most everything there, basically, that I've learned about this thing.

That is, that a person who has been to college and a person who cannot read or write can establish communication if they can have an atmosphere in which their peculiar personalities can find expression on the level of their experience. In other words, a person who has gone to school and got his Ph.D. is denied certain opportunities of living and experiences with everyday life that the man who has never gone to school has had. Without any effort to evaluate the education as you say, this person because this person is Joe Doakes has certain peculiar insights and understandings, because he is Joe Doakes, that nobody else in the world has, then you begin to get a situation in which people can talk freely. I found out there that these people not only liked these discussions, but that the crowds increased so much that when I turned in my reports, Warren H. Wilson, who was in charge of the community work, told me that I had misrepresented my figures because nobody ever got that many people out to a meeting in the mountains.

You were on the payroll at that time of . . . ?

The rural program of the Presbyterian Church. I was directly under the supervision of a man named Rev. Burton who was in charge of the Sunday School educational program. This was USA Presbyterian. I was a summer college worker. I was on their payroll for three months.

Well, that's where I got the idea for this school. That's where Highlander was born.

I can show you . . . I can show you hundreds of cards, little cards, library size, that . . . on which I used the symbol " O " . . . Ozone as a shorthand for this idea. After I had this program going, there was a lady who lived at Ozone, near the big falls, who heard about what I was doing, and said, " I have a home here and this is the kind of thing I'd like to see done. I'd like to turn my home over to you to run this kind of program here."

I said that I couldn't. I hadn't thought through it. I told her I had just discovered this thing and I wanted to think through it.

From that day on I used " O " . . . Ozone . . . for five years . . . as a symbol . . . and I always think in terms . . . a specific . . . I always thought of it as that specific community. I used " O " at Union Theological Seminary, at the University of Chicago, and in Europe. Always. It's in all my notes.

Now, that was how long before the physical establishment of Highlander?

That was before I went to Union Theological Seminary and before I worked for the Y . . . that was four years . . . I worked four years on the idea before I put it into effect. This was the germ of the idea.

All these years did you have this property here?

No. I wasn't thinking in terms of anything but that letter " O." This meant a physical location in the Southern mountains which gave me anchorage in my thinking.

Why the Southern mountains?

Because I grew up there. My people came from there.

No other reason?

Well, because I was here. That's the only answer I know. I grew up here. This is my background.

In relation to this place, where were you born?

I was born at Savannah. Down on the Tennessee River. My ancestors started out in Watauga Settlement back in 1775.

That would be in upper East Tennessee?

It was near Elizabethton. In fact, Joshua Horton got the first land grant in the Watauga Settlement which later became Tennessee, which means the first land grant in Tennessee. He got the land grant for a place called Green Hill.

That's what I call this place here. Green Hill was in the fork of the river where the big rayon plant is now. (laughter) I'm not responsible for my background.

The truth about the matter is one time when they (members of the investigating committee of the 1959 session of the Tennessee General Assembly) asked me about communism, I started to say atavism would come nearer to describing me than communism because I'm a throwback to the time when we . . . when it wasn't supposed to be a disease to be independent. See?

My grandfather was an illiterate. He grew up during the Civil War and never learned to read and write. I buried him over here. I took care of him 'til he died. He told me about these ancestors of mine. I never paid too much attention to it because I was never too much interested in it.

Three or four years ago George Mitchell, chairman of our board . . . George used to head the Southern Regional Council . . . sent me a letter saying he had run across a reference to the fact that the first slave brought into Tennessee was brought in by one of my ancestors. He asked me if I knew it. I wrote him that I vaguely remembered my grandfather mentioning it.

I started checking through some old letters that my Dad had gotten and I found this to be true. I'm proud of it . . . I think it's a good background. They were good pioneers . . . but independent.

I took this Ozone symbol and played around with it. I took notes, much to the disturbance of Reinhold Niebuhr and other people at Union Theological Seminary and Dr. Robert Park at the University of Chicago . . . in terms of what I was going to do at Ozone. Now, I didn't really mean I was going to Ozone. This was the germ of an idea. This gave me something to work out from. I started exploring educational ideas . . . up to that time I had never studied any education. I was interested . . . I majored in literature, English literature, in college. When I went to Union I was interested in religion. I was interested in comparative religions. I was interested in Bible history. Criticisms. Ethics. That general field. But I was constantly thinking in terms of what I was going to do. I had already decided after having worked for the Presbyterian Church, having worked for the state YMCA and having in that connection visited nearly every high school and college in the state, I decided I wanted to do educational work but I wasn't going to work in a regular school, but I had never heard of anything else.

So, I kept trying to find an approach, you see? an approach to this thing that wouldn't . . . that would allow me to bring people in regardless of anything and talk about anything regardless of anything. Because I thought that was the way you tapped the vitality of people. Nobody wanted to sponsor this . . . no group wanted it because they wanted to peddle their own wares . . . which is natural. . . .

At this particular point were you finding yourself quite frustrated?

Oh! Awful. Awful. That's why it took so long. I could never get this idea straight . . . every time I would move into action on it and my thinking . . . and I kind of think in action. I think in terms of rootage and a specific place . . . I think in terms of action. . . . Every time I would kind of get it to the place I wanted to use it . . . it would get fuzzy. . . . So, I decided I needed to learn a little more.

There's a wonderful person at Crossville, Tennessee, named Nightingale, Congregational minister. Retired now. I lived with him when I worked for the Presbyterian Church.

Myles Horton. PHOTO BY IDA BERMAN.

He had always had open house to people who would come
and go, including tramps. We got to be good friends. He
helped me finish college. I remember I didn't have many
clothes. Sometimes he'd give me a shirt or something . . .
maybe a pair of socks. But he did much more than that.
When I was frustrated so there, he was the one who suggested I go to Union Theological Seminary. It was through
him that I heard of Union, not through my own church which
was conservative and they thought in terms of Richmond
. . . they thought in terms of a more conservative background.

But this minister was thinking in terms of me, not in terms
of anything but what would help me as an individual develop. So, he suggested I go study with Negroes . . . Harry
F. Ward . . . Moffett was there at the time . . . wonderful
professors. . . .

He said, " They won't give you answers to your problems
but you need background." He said, " You just don't know
enough. You're just not educated well enough."

So, I went. All the time I was there I was working on
these ideas. I wasn't going to be a minister . . . I was trying to find solutions to these problems . . . and when I left
there and went to the University of Chicago to study sociology it was because I had a feeling it would help throw light
on this problem. And when, after a year in Chicago, I was offered an assistant's job with Robert Park who was head of
the sociology department, I turned it down and went to Europe. There again I thought that would help me with this
problem. Now, you ask why I went to Denmark. This is
very important. It needs to be thought of to give perspective. I was trying these ideas out on everybody. Everybody. I couldn't find many people who knew what I was

talking about. Reinhold Niebuhr, for some reason which nobody has been able to figure out, was the only professor at Union who really ever . . . really was ever sympathetic to my ideas. And not that he understood them particularly, but somehow he encouraged me and he said I was right to go ahead. He was the one person who had confidence in my ability to work this thing out. I have always been indebted to him because of that. At that period I had nothing that was easily understood.

In Chicago I ran into a Lutheran minister named Aage Møller, now in California. He was a rather unusual minister in that he had a breadth . . . more of a spiritual . . . more of a creative sense . . . more like a poet to me . . . he thought that way. He could understand me. He understood what I was groping for. He said, " Myles, what you're talking about is related to the Danish folk schools." He had grown up with these. "When I was a youngster in Denmark, I went to schools that had some of this spirit and what you should do is to . . . what you're talking about is a folk school."

I told him I had never heard of such a thing. So I read everything I could find. Then I compiled the first bibliography in the University of Chicago library on folk schools. It was made a part of the library. It was the best they had. Nobody else had done one.

I read books in French, German, and English. I read everything in the library on folk schools. I'd always read a tremendous lot anyway. I read everything I could get my hands on. In these books I found a wonderful reference to a book called . . . by John C. Campbell . . . *The Southern Highlander and His Homeland* . . . the book of that time on the Southern Appalachians . . . he did it for Russell Sage.

In that he talked about the Danish folk schools as an approach to the Southern Highlands . . . as the most appropriate educational approach for the mountaineers. I read this and all the other books and I knew it was in the general direction of my thinking . . . it had something to offer . . . but I didn't find the answers . . . I didn't . . . I found much about how wonderful the folk schools are . . . and how they did them . . . in my own mind the results they had achieved could not have been achieved by the methods they described. It didn't add up.

So, I told Augie I didn't understand this stuff. I said, " Look, I read everything I could get my hands on. It all reads wonderful, but it doesn't spell out, it doesn't add up. Because if they did what these books say they did they couldn't have gotten the results the books say they got."

He said, " Well, why don't you go over there? Find out for yourself." I said, " Well, how will I find out if those who wrote the books didn't find out? "

He said, " Well, you learn the language. Get with the people. These people who wrote these books, you know . . . they didn't dig in."

Well, it made sense to me. I had read everything I could find . . . I went through all books available on utopias . . . through everything on colonies . . . on unions . . . on co-operatives . . . I had really read everything that I thought might throw some light on my problem. I got no answers . . . so, I was willing to try anything.

This is the third year . . . after I started the idea . . . I thought I was getting old . . . I wanted to get at it . . . and I couldn't get the entire idea straight in my mind . . . so, I decided I'd . . . I'd go to Scandinavia. . . . I remember Dr. Park said . . . " Myles, if you will take a job as my assistant one year I'll guarantee to get you a scholarship to go to Europe by next year. . . . You can get your Ph.D. in the meantime . . . then you can go to Europe. . . ." I told him I couldn't wait. I wanted to go right then.

So, I worked my way. I got a job during the depression and made enough money to go to Europe. . . .

What kind of work did you do? I ask this question because I want to know what kind, what type of people your work threw you with.

Well, when I was at Union Seminary I was a director of a boys' club in the Hell's Kitchen area. Down at Christ Church. . . . It was a wonderful experience for me. . . . Anyway I was going to school not to get degrees but to learn how to do this thing . . . my idea. . . . This was my first introduction to that kind of city life . . . and I loved it. . . .

Let me interrupt you there for just a moment before we get over to Denmark. When did you discover . . . had you discovered by this time perhaps without realizing the scope of it that you were an integrationist?

Yes!

Well, when did you discover it?

I did that in college.

It is no great shakes as a story . . . but I'll tell you what happened. I grew up in a conservative church background at Savannah and then in West Tennessee . . . Humboldt . . . my parents moved to Humboldt, Tennessee . . . down there near Memphis. . . .

I went to high school in that area. And although my mother, who is still alive . . . and a very devout Christian . . . taught Sunday School classes . . . went out to the mill villages . . . and although we were poor there were still some people poorer . . . she would try to help the needy . . . she had the concept of service . . . it never was in our culture or in our philosophy to accept Negroes . . . not socially . . . we were kind . . . Negroes were not people . . . I never knew they were people . . . this was never questioned . . . churches, schools . . . everything was segregated . . . so I took for granted this was the normal pattern. I clerked in a store when I was in high school . . . I found out something . . . I found out who was paying whose bills. I got good background material . . . some of the high yellows around got their bills paid by some of the leading church people . . . and as a clerk in the store listening to gossip around I learned to put two and two together and I found out that this cleavage wasn't quite what it was supposed to be . . . see? . . . in other words there was a lot of integration going on by night. Then when I went to college I took for granted that you could be a good Christian without involving yourself in race . . . I went to college and there I was president of the Y . . . the college YMCA . . . I was very active in that . . . I was going to the Center . . . over in Nashville . . . there was a Southern YMCA college at Nashville . . . that's where the divinity school's located now . . . kind of a part of Vanderbilt . . . and I'd go to these conferences . . . and I met people from India and China . . . that was my first contact with people of different colors . . . and I thought this Chinese girl was the most beautiful girl I ever saw in my life . . . and I asked her for a date . . . later I asked her to dinner. Then I realized we couldn't go out to eat. . . .

As I said this is no great story because there is no high moral or no great ethic involved . . . it was just the plain business of being frustrated because I thought this was a good looking girl . . . yet I couldn't eat dinner with her . . .

I think that really had more to do with shaking me up than any of my background, my ideas or anything else.

It was interfering with my personal . . . my selfish, my personal desire for expression . . . they didn't haze me in college . . . I led the group that broke up hazing in college . . . I refused to be hazed . . . I organized the freshmen and we weren't hazed . . . I refused to join a fraternity . . . they said you had to join . . . so, I said I wouldn't join if you have to join . . . so, you see, I had that kind of background. . . . So, this thing bothered me you see? . . . that I couldn't take this girl to dinner with me. I didn't like to be pushed around.

Well . . . that was the first time I got a shock and I was pretty mad about it. Then later on in these same religious conferences because that was the only contact I had . . . I grew up with them . . . I met a Negro . . . a Negro man . . . a very fine fellow . . . he seemed to be a little offbeat in his ideas . . . a little more imaginative and creative than some of the other people around . . . and I got switched around on that. . . .

Up to that time I didn't have any feeling . . . I probably mouthed all these things about brotherhood like everybody else but it didn't mean anything. It was only through being limited in my own desire for expression that this came to me as a rude shock . . . you know . . . that you couldn't do this thing . . . then I got to questioning it intellectually, ethically and morally . . . but that's how it happened . . . well, after that I guess I just developed normally . . . somehow I had enough understanding to know that I couldn't have rights just for me . . . there were no rights just for me alone . . . and it didn't take me very long to generalize on this experience to the place where if I was going to be free to take a Chinese girl into a restaurant . . . then everybody

35

would have to be free to do the same . . . and not only a
Chinese girl but a girl of still another color or race . . . I
made it more or less an operating principle that nobody could
have their rights interfered with as long as they were tending
to their own business . . . which I thought I was . . . that's
how I got in it . . . now I don't mean to minimize the fact
that I had grown up on a New Testament . . . Old Testament background . . . and had that background to fall back
on . . . later on I led several fights in Tennessee for integration . . . in fact when I was student YMCA secretary they
were as glad to have me resign as I was to resign after a year
. . . I had interracial meetings all over the state . . . I had
interracial Hi-Y club meetings at the Farragut Hotel in Knoxville in 1929 . . . no segregation . . . I did it all over the
state . . . I didn't ask anybody anything . . . I did it.

So, I got into that fairly early . . . but through no great
idealism or anything . . . just the interference with my de-
sires . . . I'm not apologetic about it. . . .

Now, after these experiences . . . I never gave up . . .
I didn't want to be segregated. As a mountaineer I was segregated from people who weren't mountaineers . . . as a
country boy I was segregated from city people . . . I didn't
like any kind of segregation . . . I never thought of it as
race . . . segregation to me is anybody who is being excluded . . . and I happen to be . . . to come from a poor
background . . . I had a hard time when I was growing up
. . . I was excluded from a lot of things . . . I was excluded
because I didn't have clothes . . . I was excluded because I
didn't have money enough . . . fifty cents to go to a . . . a
. . . I never will forget it . . . a violin concert. I've been
excluded for a lot of reasons . . . I don't like to be excluded!
I'm also opposed to the segregation of ideas . . . I just don't
believe in segregation . . . I don't care what it is . . . I never

One of Highlander's first students, a typical resident of Grundy County.

pulled any punches about it either . . . I fought it . . . I refused to join any organization that set me apart from anybody else . . . just like I refuse to go to church now because I can't take Negroes with me . . . just a matter of principle with me . . . and practice. Well, anyhow when I went to the University of Chicago, I did . . . I got into research . . . there I met a psychiatrist . . . Ames . . . he's dead now . . . and . . . I met him because I got into an argument with him . . . he was talking about . . . he thought that the unemployed were maladjusted . . . so I asked how long would it take a person to get maladjusted? Can you get maladjusted all at once or is it a long process . . . how do you account for the fact that there are a million more maladjusted people than last year . . . he ducked this question . . . after the lecture was over he said he wanted to see me . . . through this we got to be pretty good friends . . . and he wanted some help on some articles . . . wanted me to look up references . . . and I took the job with him for which I got fabulous pay . . . the reason I got fabulous pay is that he had five people working for him and I asked him if I could do all their work would I get their pay . . . he said yes and I took their jobs.

I went to Denmark, and having already read everything I could find, I decided I was going to learn the language. This was important. I couldn't have done anything without it. I'm very poor at languages so I worked out my own system. I amazed people. I tried a course in Danish and then transferred to a course in English. I found out they taught more Danish in this class than in the Danish class. Also, I went to see plays in Danish. I'd get newspapers and just sit there and stare at them, picking out a word here and there. Pretty soon I began to be able to use a few words. Then I moved into the home of a Danish family. Then I met a very beautiful girl and started taking dancing lessons. That was a phony. I couldn't dance and didn't care much about it. But she taught me to speak Danish.

I would go to lectures in Danish and just sit there. Pretty soon I could tell what was being said. So, after about four months, when I was about broke, I had learned enough Danish to lecture myself. I talked about America. Of course I knew a lot of things to talk about because they knew just about nothing about America.

I visited all the schools . . . folk schools, that is . . . in the country. I remember going to one of these schools and telling the man in charge I wanted to sit in on his school for a while as an observer. In a very tired and uninterested manner he asked me to come on in. One of the maids came in. I spoke to her in Danish. The old man heard me and asked if I spoke the language. I told him I could speak a little and understand him if he didn't speak too fast. His wife didn't speak English and this was the first time she had ever talked with an American. They loved me and were anxious to have me at the school. I started to question him about the purpose of the schools. To simplify his reply, he said the folk schools were set up to deal with problems that deeply involved the people in times of a crisis. Reading, writing, and arithmetic were not aims of these schools. They dealt with, for the most part, adults who had reached an age where they could think for themselves. First school was on the border of Germany. It was for Danism and against Germanism. Another was . . . for the peasant against the nobility. . . . Then there was another which stood for . . . lightness against darkness . . . religious training aimed at removing the sternness of Calvinism from the religious training and education. Each of these schools had a purpose . . . and they clarified that purpose by saying what they were for and what they were against. . . . Then the teaching grew out of the people . . . the situations they were in . . . but their methodology was no good from my point of view . . . they use a lot of lectures and a lot of preaching. . . .

Everybody had described this in the books I had read and that's why I couldn't understand how they got what they got with the methods they used . . . well, they got it in spite of them not because of them. This man taught me that people must express themselves through the living word . . . that's the concept they use . . . the emotional feeling of the person . . . the person himself believes . . . that's a sound idea . . . that you must believe deeply in what you're teaching or you can't teach . . . in adult education.

I rejected the methodology. I think we know much more about this in our country. But I did learn this much . . . I got clarification on . . . against my background of being neutral . . . you have to know what you're for . . . you have to believe in what you're for . . . you have to deal with people as they are and you deal with the crisis. You deal with situations in which people are most involved . . . I got some very powerful things from these people. . . . You need to clarify your own thinking by knowing what your enemies are for but you must not magnify your opposition by putting it on a level with what you are for. . . . I think that leads to too much emotional and intellectual energy going to what you dislike and what you hate rather than constructively using it for what you're for. I say . . . I am for democracy . . . I am for brotherhood . . . now there are barriers in the way . . . I will stop . . . I am stopped by getting rid of the barriers to keep people from organizing . . . because in a democratic society you can have people organized in labor unions . . . if there is no organization then there is a barrier keeping me from my goal . . . you have to deal with your barriers . . . I don't spend time thinking I'm against . . . I'm violently against no unions . . . let's say I'm for getting rid of this barrier . . . which means I'm for unions. Now, take integration . . . I am for integration because if there is segregation . . . it keeps me from my goal . . . I mean I just think better that way . . . I'm against the negative . . . I'm for the positive. . . .

One Christmas night . . . I'll never forget this . . . I had planned to leave for a lecture tour in Germany. . . . We were having a family party . . . that's the way they do things in Denmark . . . good food . . . wine. . . . Some of us took a walk toward a church . . . a beautiful church there. . . . We sat on a stone wall and listened to the chimes and singing. . . . Then we came back. . . . I took my girl home . . . then went to bed but couldn't sleep . . . wide awake . . . everything was right with the world . . . I tried to read a little. . . . All at once . . . I said to myself . . . my god . . . four years . . . all you do is get a place . . . and move in . . . you're there . . . the situation is there . . . the situation is there . . . you start with this and let it grow . . . you have your ideas . . . you know your goal . . . it will build its own structure and take its own form . . . no wonder you can't figure it out . . . you shouldn't be able to . . . purpose and situation depend on factors that you can't know anything about . . . forget all the methods . . . find the place . . . the people . . . the situation . . . use your ideas as your lodestone and move into the thing and start. . . . So I wrote on the side of my bed . . . " go to O . . . find the place . . . move in and start living with the people and teach the people whatever they want to be taught but in the light of your ideas. . . ." And that's all there is to it . . . there's nothing else to it . . . I wrote it all down . . . about 4 o'clock I finally went to sleep. . . .

The goal was . . . brotherhood and democracy . . . those two things . . . and I've been very careful not to define them . . . there's no blueprint. . . . I've never philosophized about them . . . in the sense of saying . . . " this is it . . ." I've said they're growing . . . ever-growing concepts . . . they are changing concepts . . . instead of goal posts they're arrows pointing in a direction . . . giving one direction . . . give you a lot of leeway . . . and my conception of brotherhood and democracy grows every day . . . and society's conception grows every day. Democracy in Athens was different from democracy today . . . why should I define democracy? Let's say it's clear enough . . . and when I talk about democracy and brotherhood I mean traditional American democratic concepts and traditional Biblical concepts . . . I don't mean anything more than the basic things I got there . . . but, brother, I believe it's open ended . . . it keeps moving . . . as you get closer to it you see more. Now once I decided that I didn't have any intellectual problems . . . since that day I've never had an intellectual problem . . . I've tried to be effective in terms of the situation . . . in terms of method . . . I've tried to be an educator in other words . . . methods must fit the situation.

Well, I started home then . . . the people I lived with loaned me the money. . . .

I got to New York and had ten cents when I got off the boat . . . used a nickel to call this doctor I'd worked with (Dr. Ames) . . . used the other nickel to pay subway fare to his home . . . borrowed five dollars from him . . . then I went to see Niebuhr . . . I told him I had it . . . told him I knew what I wanted to do. . . . He said my time in Denmark was well spent. . . . I told him I needed money to get this thing going. . . . He wrote the first letter requesting funds . . . this was in 1932. . . . We talked about the

needs of the day . . . the need for labor organizations . . .
the AFL then was at a low ebb . . . 2,000,000 members
maybe . . . neither the AFL nor the Communist Party
which had unions at that time . . . would offer any help in
this thing . . . we had to work out more democratic union
forms . . . that was in the first letter sent out.

The first contribution ever made was from Sherwood
Eddy . . . I had met him before . . . Niebuhr called him
and made an appointment for me . . . I went down to see
him . . . he was a very busy man . . . I went to his office
. . . he was going somewhere else . . . he was just leaving
. . . he said, " Let's just walk along Broadway . . ." I talked
as we walked and explained to him I wanted to start this
thing in the Southern mountains . . . I told him I thought
this was the best place to start . . . I told him heavy industry was coming . . . I told him I had seen War Department
maps for power development . . . forerunner of TVA. . . .
He said I was working in the future a long time. . . . I answered that my ideas were for the future . . . there had to
be a starting point. . . . So, we walked and talked . . .
then he said, " Well, if Niebuhr says he has known you
for three or four years I have to take this on faith. But, if
you're recommended by Niebuhr I suppose it's all right.
He's never recommended anything to me yet that wasn't
sound."

We talked on still more . . . he shook his head . . .
then he said, "Well, I'm going to give you a hundred dollars.
This is the first time I ever gave a penny to an idea walking
down Broadway."

I'll never forget that . . . " an idea for something in the
Southern mountains walking down Broadway. . . ." And he
gave me the $100. It was the first money I ever got for this
thing.

All but three of the original contributors to the school are still alive and still giving to the school.

So, that's how I got started. . . .

So, we didn't set any classes . . . we just offered services . . . we just said that whatever the people wanted that we could do we would do. . . . In the first class was a woman who lived near here who wanted to know about child psychology . . . I told her I didn't know anything about it but that we would find out what she wanted to know. . . .

I came down and went back to stay with Nightingale . . . he said he knew a Dr. Lillian Johnson who owned some property and was getting ready to retire . . . she wanted to turn her property over to someone for a good cause . . . she wasn't for unions . . . she came from a banking family in Memphis . . . she was one of the first women college prexys . . . at a college in Ohio . . . was a suffragette . . . helped set up credit unions . . . sent abroad by Wilson . . . she started the county fair here. . . . She did a lot of good but she was a little aristocratic . . . neighbors used to say that Dr. Johnson would say, "Pull off your shoes and come in," showing her aristocratic side. That was her concept of being a service to the people. I didn't have such problems. I had grown up poor.

Well, she had some misgivings, particularly when we got mixed up in a strike at Wilder, Tennessee, the next year and got branded as Communists . . . in a big way . . . up to that time they thought I was a Catholic because I was in here without having any formal program. . . .

I went over to Wilder to see what was going on . . . I found they were misusing Red Cross funds. . . . Troopers were in there terrorizing strikers and their families . . . shooting . . . I spent the day over there getting information . . . wrote an article for one of the papers . . . I thought the tactics were awful . . . so, I was arrested . . . I was charged with " getting information and going back and teaching it. . . ." That was the official charge . . . by State Guards and Highway Patrol. . . . They took me to head-quarters there . . . they had John Dewey's book on the school and society there . . . I picked it up and started read-ing it . . . about midnight the head officer came in and said this is all a mistake . . . you weren't really arrested . . . we're sorry. . . .

I said . . . " The hell I wasn't . . . they took bayonets and marched me down here . . . if it hadn't been for them I'd been gone . . . I was going back to Crossville. . . ."

The officer said I could go . . . I said, " In this rain? No buses, no transportation. No, I'm going to stay right here." He wouldn't let me so I made him take me to the hotel and get me a room.

Mr. Horton, what year was your first conference or work-shop held here?

As soon as we got here [1933], we started having people in. For the first year we worked mainly with the local peo-ple . . . because we didn't have any way of getting out . . . we didn't have much money . . . they weren't on labor unions . . . they were concerned with their immediate prob-lems . . . unemployed people wanting to know how to start . . . how they could have co-op gardens . . . we discussed co-op . . . people came two hours a day five days a week. We organized a co-op for them . . . they came to hear about other parts of the world . . . mainly I would show them pic-tures and tell them where I'd been . . . sharing some of these things with them . . . they would share their prob-lems with me . . . then we started bringing people in . . . Highlander has always had a very small staff . . . we've

45

concentrated on bringing in what today you would call consultants . . . one of the first people who was brought in was Charles Johnson . . . president of Fisk University . . . he and Mrs. Johnson were the first Negroes to spend the night here. That was the first year of the school . . . others came in . . . people from Wilder started coming in . . . people heard about us in the mine, textile mills and elsewhere and came in. . . .

How about some of the top labor leaders of the day?

Well, at that time, at the very beginning there were very few labor leaders who were anything more than business agents for the craft unions . . . so, we had a strike here the first year of the school . . . a woodcutters strike . . . bugwood cutter's strike . . . people were cutting wood to be used for its acid content . . . they were getting 75 cents a day working eight to ten hours a day. They started coming here for meetings and asked about wages in other places . . . about unions. . . . I told them first about this county. Knights of Labor organized in this county about 1891–92. They had convicts working in the mines . . . the meeting of the miners to lay plans to get rid of the convicts were held in this house . . . this is the oldest house on the mountain . . . was a meeting place for Knights of Labor . . . so, I started out telling them about the labor history of their own county . . . I got interested in John R. Commons . . . labor history. I found other people to come in, local people, to talk about this history and the problems . . . we asked state AFL leadership to help us out . . . but we didn't get much help. . . . In 1934 the UMW official from Jellico came down here when NRA came in . . . he stopped by . . . he said he was going to organize mine workers in area . . . in a few hours he came back and said he had one started . . . then he came in

and asked if I would guide them and help them get started
. . . he asked me if I would organize the CIO in Tennessee
. . . he was Bill Turnblazer. . . . Well, since then we have
had literally hundreds of the top labor leaders here . . .
from this point on we closely allied with labor unions . . .
we were identified with the industrial unions because of our
association with UMW and our philosophy . . . Highlander
got well labeled as a CIO organization. I did a lot of work
for the minority resolution . . . we ran the first official CIO
school here for four years before there was another in the
U.S. We ran it for the Southern Regional office. . . . So, in
that period the school, Highlander, was involved in the labor
movement as it is involved in the integration movement today . . . and it was just as unpopular then as this is unpopular now . . . it was against the times . . . the methods we
use will fit most any situation . . . any aim. . . .

The FBI has been checking on Highlander since it started
. . . it all started in 1932 . . . I was told that by the FBI. . . .
They would come by and ask questions . . . one fellow
came by and caused such a row with the unions he was transferred from the state . . . then came a Harvard graduate
and used quite different tactics . . . he was a nice fellow
. . . he explained that the FBI has to investigate all complaints . . . he said there's an organizer down in Georgia
. . . and the sheriff said he (the organizer) was a Highlander student and a Communist and was down there trying
to start a revolution . . . I told him that if the organizer was
with the Butchers' Union from Chicago as he said he was,
then he had never been to Highlander . . . and he sure as
hell is not starting a revolution . . . I told him he was just
an organizer . . . I told him that he not only wouldn't start
a revolution but if he was like most of the Butchers' organizers he wouldn't even start a union. About three months

later the same FBI agent came back . . . he said this is
worse than the other . . . he asked, "Have you been . . .
have you had any rifle practice around here?"

"What do you mean?"

"You know. Training for an attempt to overthrow the
government by violence?"

"No. What are you getting at?"

"Well, I got a report that some targets . . . guns. . . ."

"No, I don't know about any training to overthrow the
government."

"Can't you think of anything that might have caused
such a report?"

I thought a while and then it came to me. . . .

I said, "We had a reunion here about a month ago. One
of the fellows brought a .22 rifle along . . . he went out on
the bluff back of the place to shoot . . . he shot five or six
boxes of shells. . . ."

The agents went out to look at the scene. . . .

*Was Highlander at any time a target for the Un-American
Activities Committee under Martin Dies?*

Dies first mentioned . . . was the first to mention Highlander . . . he used Paul Crouch's testimony . . . as best as
I remember. . . . I proposed to Dies in a letter that he hold
a public investigation to get the thing straightened out. . . .
It was never held. . . .

Later I was called before the Internal Security Committee in New Orleans. . . . It was a one-man hearing. . . . I
gave Eastland a prepared statement.

I told him I organized the Workers Alliance. . . . He
asked if I didn't know it was a Communist organization. . . .
I told him I knew it wasn't because I wrote David Lasser a
letter and told him I wouldn't have anything to do with any-

48

thing connected with the Communists. . . . He wanted to know if I had written letters on certain legislators in Congress . . . I told him I didn't know but if he would refresh my memory I would answer his questions. . . .

He never put my statement in the record . . . I never got a transcript of the hearing which he promised . . . what year was this . . . four years ago. He asked about Jim Dombrowski [a prominent Highlander staff member] . . . I told him I let others speak for themselves, I speak for myself. He insisted that I answer the question. . . . I told him he had let known Communists talk and asked why couldn't I. . . . He said to the U.S. Marshals present, "Throw him out! Throw him out! . . ." They stood right behind me . . . they grabbed me . . . wanted me to struggle . . . I gritted my teeth and kept a straight face . . . they took me in the hall and threw me on the stone floor. One said Eastland said I was a dangerous character and not to take any chances. . . . It was all set up . . . it was quite obvious. . . . He threatened to get me for contempt . . . he never did . . . he didn't have any reason to . . . Highlander has never been on any subversive list. . . . The FBI has cleared us . . . at least the Justice Department has never taken any action. . . .

. . . When the Eastland hearing came up I was told unless I took the Fifth I may have to go to jail . . . I refused to talk about others and also refused to take the Fifth . . . I wouldn't use it because it would be used against the school . . . I chose to operate on the First Amendment instead . . . I told my children what might happen . . . I wanted them to know in advance . . . the children said they wouldn't want me to do anything to hurt Highlander . . . they are accustomed to having to face criticism when you stand on principle. . . .

I've sworn under oath that I am not and never have been

49

a Communist . . . nobody has ever challenged me as being a Communist. . . . To my knowledge, I've never had an associate who is or was a Communist. . . .

Returning from Denmark . . . how much Russian History did you know? How familiar were you with Communist philosophy at that time?

I didn't know much . . . I had studied some Hegel. . . . In the beginning my primary concern was economics . . . I got very little out of Marx's writing . . . I got much more out of Hamilton . . . The Federalist Papers. . . .

Communism to me . . . I don't want to minimize it as a world force . . . it is a world force . . . I just don't agree with it . . . it has weaknesses but it is important . . . very important . . . I wouldn't be a party to working with labor unions unless in reality those labor unions ran their own programs . . . nobody has a right to go into a trade union and use a union for any other purpose . . . I had no right to use it for Highlander, for the Presbyterian Church nor the Communist Party . . . in other words you cannot take a labor organization and subvert it to something else . . . I've fought and bled on these principles . . . it is these things I dislike about the Communist Party. . . .

However, I said Communists shouldn't be barred from the Southern Conference for Human Welfare. . . I wanted to have the organization open to all . . . America is not endangered by Communism . . . Americans will never go for it . . . our traditions are against it. . . .

I have quoted Myles Horton at great length, because his ideas, his personality, and his experiences are fundamental to an understanding of Highlander and because it's important to hear the solitary voice of a man speaking and answering with simple honesty, about the things that are important to him. *Vox clamantis in deserto* was the motto of an educational institution I once inhabited, a slogan usually mistranslated as *A voice crying out in the wilderness*, which only goes to show how carelessly most people read any book, including the Good One.

What it really says is *The voice of ONE crying out in the wilderness*, and the *one* is the point. This is what Myles Horton has always been, a unique human voice, speaking out of our wilderness in the direction of our hope.

After Myles' return from Denmark he proceeded rapidly, as he has indicated, to translate Ozone into a physical reality. His contact with Dr. Lillian Johnson at precisely the right time for both of them was a stroke of pure luck; but the way he took advantage of the opportunity was pure Horton. His original partner in the enterprise was Don West, a young Congregationalist minister who had also visited Denmark to study its folk schools. After concluding an arrangement with Dr. Johnson, they moved into her farmhouse in November, 1932, and began to develop the program outlined by Myles in the preceding interview.

It was a hard first winter. There was very little money, and the school had to make itself known to the people of Grundy County from scratch. But mountain folk are friendly, if you're not an outsider, and Myles was one of their own people. With the elemental wisdom which is his genius, he let things develop at their own pace, and let the program grow out of the people's problems, not out of his own ideas about them. Discussions led to informal courses; informal courses led to bringing in consultants, the beginning of the workshops we shall see in action later. The need for food resulted in the establishment of an agricultural co-op, not a very successful one but one which helped bring the people

51

closer together. The bugwood strike, to be described later, produced another sortie into community organization, and a visit from strikers at Wilder, a labor conflict also to be described later, led to the school's first field work and to a course in economics.

All this is explicit in the interview we have just seen; what is more important is that implicit in this document is the whole future course of Highlander. All of Highlander's basic activities were gotten underway that winter; in a very real sense the remainder of this book is an elaboration of themes which Myles has himself already stated for us.

When, a year after its opening, the school was officially incorporated, other changes had taken place. New staff members had arrived, notably James Dombrowski, who had come down from Union Theological Seminary and was to bear a considerable portion of the administrative load at Highlander for years. Don West had decided to move on to his native Georgia. The school, now solidly entrenched in the community, was on its way toward becoming the potent influence throughout the South that it has been for the past thirty-five years. It had established a unified program whose three chief thrusts, community organization, labor education, and integration, were never to be separate.

John Dewey, that wise old philosopher-educator, recognized this as early as 1933, when he wrote on September 27:

Having talked with Dr. Dombrowski and gone over with him the work and plans of the Highlander Folk School, I wish to say that I am much impressed with the intelligence and sincerity and devotion of the plan and those who are engaged in carrying it out. It is one of the most hopeful social-educational plans I know of.

It was a plan, yes, and an idea. But Highlander has always been an idea in *action* — as we shall see.

CHAPTER TWO

Attacks

Highlander has always been under attack.

A prime delusion of our mechanized society is that the United States is an eminently Christian nation dedicated to peace, goodwill, and the brotherhood of man. The fact that this is a myth does not trouble a people for whom history has become a miasma called social studies. That the prince of peace, a country boy named Jesus, founded the most warlike religion in the memory of man does not appear in our textbooks. Nor does the fact that America has set the world's record for wars, civil and other, in the brief while we have endured under the sun we now threaten to eclipse.

The pursuit of happiness has never been our goal. We are a rough, violent people, children of a lost frontier, conceived in rebellion and dedicated to the proposition that the way to get one up fastest is to hate first. We are the most human of all countries, and the most terrifying. It is no accident that our most popular television shows feature gun fights, whether western, cops and robbers, or international espionage; situation comedies where the man is always a fool; and medical dramas whose core is death. We live by hate and its denial. No other country ever conceived of morticians or sanitary engineers; pretty terms for ugliness are the way we think about things.

Bombs for Peace!

And we believe it.

Violence is our way of life, as all the rest of the world knows. It's a fact we have a genius for reminding them of.

If you want to understand a people, learn their jokes. In America you'll find that all men are idiots. The boys come home to suburbia and laugh at television shows that demonstrate how their wives wear the pants. Lucille Ball, God help us, is the mother of us all. But no woman has ever been elected President, and lady Senators are in short supply.

But we cherish our illusions. We have to.

We live by them.

We're the Romans of the new West, unimaginative, technically handy, and ignorant. We're trying to create a Pax Americana and failing miserably. We lack the same thing the Romans lacked, and we'll probably go down the same drain. We don't understand people because we don't understand ourselves. *Veni, vidi, vici* was the Roman formula, but it didn't work. The barbarians won out, and made our world.

Which brings us back to America. And Highlander.

The Romans lived on hate too. They lived by it, and in the end they died by it. Nowadays the weapons are more sophisticated but the pattern is the same. Delusion.

Is there any hope?

Not much, maybe, but it's real, and it exists in the most improbable place: In the South, and Highlander epitomizes it.

We have one advantage over the Romans. This country was founded on a revolutionary idea. The Romans borrowed most of their ideas, including their gods, from the

Greeks, and we borrowed ours too, from the English Puritans and the French Encyclopedists. But we had the happy chance of beginning in retreat and rebellion, a happenstance that spilled tea in Boston and propelled the conservative George Washington, wooden teeth and all, into open revolt. We had no option. We were running brave and scared.

The Romans murdered a sophisticated society, the Etruscans, and they did it with their customary thoroughness, to the point that the Etruscans' marvelous art has taken two thousand years to begin to be recovered and their language is still indecipherable. We raped a virgin continent inhabited by a deliberately primitive people — foreigners too, from the days a man could walk across Bering Strait — whose life was ideally adapted to the open country of our marvelous home.

But we weren't afraid of the Indians. Despite the folklore which is now institutionalized in television, the Indians never had a chance, and we knew it from the start. No bow and arrow was ever a match for a gun, as stout Cortez proved in Mexico, to his eternal shame.

It was the English who scared the pants off us. They were hurting us in the place where it matters to Americans, in the pocketbook, and the wisest of the American conservatives declared rebellion. I say the wisest, because the more practical did not. The Tories remained staunchly loyal to the Crown. Like their successors, the John Birchers, they thought they knew which side their bread was buttered on.

Only they didn't know a thing.

Tom Jefferson was right. Even John Hancock, that conservative Bostonian who had to be brainwashed to commit his signature in the only place that would ever immortalize him, knew better. He knew, finally, that it was time to *do*.

Of course the Founding Fathers neglected to write the

Bill of Rights into the Constitution, thus laying the groundwork for the most opprobrious epithet in American history, "Fifth-Amendment Communist." But they corrected that soon enough, to the distaste of those who continue to insist that America is a Republic, not a Democracy. The English translation here is that there's no Democracy for Negroes or whites who think like the Founding Fathers did.

"Two things I hates," a decrepit Southern Congressman once proclaimed when segregation had begun to be a political issue," Segregation and Niggers on the Beach." I thought about him once when I got a phone call from an irate, God-fearing citizen of Vermont who wanted some information about the ineffectual teaching of mathematics in this country — that was before the halcyon days of the New Math, but that's another story. I explained that my organization had just published a book on the subject and that he could communicate with the senior author at Delano Junior High School in Chicago.

"You mean the middle name of that *scoundrel* in the White House?" he asked.

This was fifteen years after FDR's death, but I agreed. In his terms he was right.

That's what White Citizens' Councils are about, and what Highlander has always been against. The right word here is *for*, because Highlander has always been a positive force, as Myles Horton so eloquently stated. *For*, that is, the things the Councils and my friend from Vermont are *against*.

Myles Horton is a great man in a great tradition. He encompasses all the good things in the real American Dream, and he has never wavered from this faith. People like this ask for attacks. And they get them.

For a very specific reason, I begin our story of Highlander

in action with an account of attacks upon the school. As we shall see, the violence and frequency of these attacks have been extraordinary. Small and poverty-stricken as it has been, Highlander has from the beginning managed to throw the defenders of bigotry and intolerance into an uproar. You can tell a good deal about an institution from its enemies, and Highlander has always had the right ones. You can also generally estimate an organization's effectiveness by the virulence with which these enemies attack it. There are, of course, exceptions, notably the American Communist Party, an impressively ineffectual force in American life for many years, whose chief function has now become to provide a label which can be pinned on organizations like Highlander when they seek to bring about democratic changes in the status quo.

Highlander, however, committed to a radical belief in democracy and opposed to segregation or authoritarianism of any sort, has followed the classic pattern of developing appropriate enemies on the basis of its own performance. As a result, the attacks launched upon it are, in many ways, the most revealing part of its history.

As early as 1933, a year after Highlander was founded, it was under attack by an official of the Central Labor Union in Knoxville, Tennessee. From the vantage of 1968, this seems an unlikely probability to the uninformed. In fact it wasn't. (I had the same experience in the same year in Louisville, Kentucky, where a local of which I was vice-president was sold down the river by a red-faced National President from Boston.) In 1933 the craft unions were fighting for their lives, and an organization like Highlander, which got out and actually stirred up the workers and by philosophy was opposed to the craft union idea, was not a popular institution with them. The boys in the shiny blue suits couldn't care less about workers, but they cared plenty about their weekly paychecks.

The fink in Knoxville was Frank J. Torlay, a union official who accused three Highlander staff members of being atheists and Communists.

Here's what the Central Labor Council reported:

. . . The defendant [Mr. Torlay] . . . pleaded guilty to the charge of publicly characterizing Miss Zilla Hawes as a Communist and an atheist and reiterated this charge in the trial. The defendant denied making any such charge against Mr. Franz Daniel or Mr. Jack Coope, and the committee heard the prosecution in support of the charges on this point.

. . . The prosecutors in the case presented their pleas and evidence in a candid and fair manner, their deportment was courteous and their testimony open and frank in every respect. . . .

In contrast to the open, frank, and candid demeanor and testimony of the prosecutors, the defendant in this case was evasive, arrogant, and flippant in his attitude toward the charges and the questions of the committee, and in some respects insulting in his deportment. The defendant refused to answer fair and pertinent questions categorically and seemed to take delight in the status of what is commonly known as a " smart " witness.

In answer to the demand of the committee that he submit proof of his charge that Miss Hawes is a Communist and an atheist, the defendant admitted that he had no proof, and exhibited an arrogant and defiant attitude toward the committee's efforts to extract from him some reasonable ground for this charge.

. . . While the preponderance of evidence supported the charges of Mr. Daniel and Mr. Coope that the defendant had charged them with being Communists and atheists, the defendant denied that he had ever made these charges. Yet the fact remains that the defendant gave an interview to the paper, along with the copies of the charges, and all of the prosecutors' names were linked with this story, and Mr. Daniel and Mr. Coope, against whom the defendant disclaimed making any charges,

Typical children's toys in Appalachia during the depression.

were equally hurt, they and their work, along with Miss Hawes, by the publication of the story. . . .

The defendant in this case admits that he has no proof that any of the prosecution is a Communist, a red, or an atheist, yet it is proved by his own admission and the evidence of creditable witnesses that he advised the textile workers of Lenoir City to "run them out of town with rotten eggs. . . ."

The committee finds that the prosecutors have proved their charges in every respect. There is no indication that the prosecutors are anything less than honest, decent, loyal union people. This committee finds them completely justified in their charges and their conduct in every respect worthy of the confidence and faith of organized labor. This committee finds in this case the interests of the prosecutors and the interests of organized labor identical, and declares that the defendant in this case has acted contrary to all recognized union honor and practice, and that he has done labor a great and monstrous injury by his false and malicious charges against the prosecutors.

Miss Zilla Hawes, in particular, deserves the sympathy and consideration of the Central Labor Union in this situation. This is a new day and a new era, in which the womanhood of America is taking step with the manhood in the labor movement, to build a new and better unionism for the workers of America, and it is a responsibility of organized labor to welcome and aid the efforts of these women who are following in the footsteps of the pioneer women labor leaders, and who are in a sense pioneers themselves.

Miss Hawes came to Knoxville and made great progress in her work until the natural enemies of the labor movement began their usual scurrilous attacks upon her aims and motives. This, however, was to be expected, because we are familiar with the lying attacks of the enemies of organized labor who seek to alienate the unorganized worker from the leaders who preach the doctrine of unionism.

When Miss Hawes came as a delegate to the Central Labor Union, and she and her delegation were enthusiastically cheered by the members of this body, and she was accorded just and deserved recognition of her services, organized labor took a stand.

There are two morals to this story. One is that Highlander, whose interests have always been in democracy and people, has never minded whose toes it stepped on. Here it was a union official's who had a good thing going with the mill owners. The workers were caught in the middle, and Highlander stepped right into the middle of the middle. Result — the usual attack from those whose interests were threatened and support from those whose interests Highlander was defending, the strikers.

The other is that a council of conservative craft unions who had many reasons not to love Highlander, which from the beginning was committed to the industrial union idea, nevertheless respected the efficiency and integrity of Highlander's work — here exemplified in the person of Zilla Hawes. The interesting thing is that, for all the name-calling, none of the many attackers of the school have ever questioned its effectiveness. It has been precisely this efficiency, and the threat to their particular entrenched interests, that has frightened them. The idea has *worked.*

Later Highlander was to come under attack from the competing CIO, whose existence it did more than anyone else to make possible in the South, and for similar reasons. The school was then insisting on more democracy in unions that had begun to lose it. It's a small world.

A more sensational episode featured, among others, Dillard King, a local boy. He got involved while walking along the road, which goes to prove how dangerous it is not to own a Cadillac, even in Monteagle. Dillard, a former leader in the bugwood strike and the organization of the WPA workers in Grundy County, events to which we will return, was footing it along the highway one afternoon, just heading wherever he had a mind to head, when he came across a fellow sitting on the side of the road. He was a city type,

The main building at Highlander Folk School.

plump and obviously uncomfortable, and he asked Dillard the way to Highlander School. Dillard was a Monteagle boy with the quiet manners of the mountain people, but he had also been around. He'd quit school at eighteen and gone to Chicago and worked at odd jobs for three months until he discovered, quicker than a lot of Cumberland folk in the thirties, that there was no permanent work there. So he came back, took to cutting bugwood at 75¢ a day, helped lead an abortive but educational strike and then, when Highlander helped organize the WPA workers, became financial secretary of a local.

So he knew about outlanders and was ready, a classic good Samaritan, to help the one he found by the side of the road. He was a good man, Dillard, and he was also just the kind of man the stranger was looking for. He answered questions politely and accurately and when the stranger explained that he was a Texas schoolteacher with a stomach-ache, he was particularly considerate in getting him to Highlander Folk School, which has never turned away a serious visitor, regardless of race, color, creed, or politics. This fact will become important later.

Highlander's only requirement was that any visitor identify himself honestly. Communists, Mohammedans, Shinto-ists were equally welcome: they just had to say who they were.

The stranger, a reporter for the Nashville *Tennessean*, found it inconvenient to comply with this requirement; even his name was faked. He'd have been welcome if he'd just said who he was, and the facilities of the school would have been available to him. They were anyway, but to be honest about it would have voided the cloak and dagger operation, which any normal television viewer can tell you is essential to successful spying. So John McDougal Burns, posing as

John McDougal, spent two days acquiring information he could have gotten for the price of a cup of coffee back at the ranch in Nashville, where many of his colleagues knew the school intimately, and went home to write a series of sensational exposés.

But let's let Myles describe the incident first, before we take a look at one of Burns' offerings.

Myles wrote:

The *Nashville Tennessean* ran six front page articles under four column headlines, each longer than President Roosevelt's Jackson Day dinner speech, attacking the Highlander Folk School. (October 15–20, 1939) The School was charged with being "a center, if not the center for the spreading of Communism in thirteen Southeastern states!" Proof ranged from operating a nursery school to helping elect a sheriff. The Community Council, made up of representatives of the churches, grammar school, Parent Teachers Association, unions, and cooperatives was viewed with alarm. "One of the oddest things I have ever run across," wrote the reporter-detective. "At their meetings they sing old folk songs" and then take up "the problems of the Community." The discovery of the *Daily Worker* among the forty newspapers in the reading room made additional proof unnecessary. Throughout the articles and accompanying editorials the words "communist" and "progressive" were used interchangeably.

These startling disclosures were made by John McDougal Burns, who according to an editorial in the *Tennessean* (October 22) "is an experienced and accurate newspaperman in whose reports the readers can have full confidence." The purpose of his articles, continued the editorial, was "to turn the light on the activities of this center of leftist teaching . . ." The assignment was made by Mr. Silliman Evans, president and publisher of the paper. Plans for the "exposure" were kept secret from the reporters and editors, many of whom had visited the school or were acquainted with its purpose. Letters of protest were not handled through the regular channels, but, with the exception of

a few that were published under pressure, were destroyed by the
" front office."

The procedure followed by Burns was somewhat irregular
and a few inaccuracies were allowed to creep in, due, no doubt,
to the difficulty of the assignment. According to the reporter he
was sent to find out about " Communism " and " Moscow " at a
southern labor school in the Tennessee mountains. The articles
were introduced by a statement that the " experienced and accurate newspaperman " spent ten days at the school and in Grundy
County. Actually the reporter was our guest for only two days.
By using an assumed name, posing as a Texas college professor
suffering with a stomachache, and claiming to have been sent by
a cousin (a fellow-reporter on the *Tennessean* who had spoken
at the school as a representative of the Newspaper Guild) Burns
managed somehow to get into the school — a feat matched by
only five hundred other visitors during 1939.

Special mention should be made of the " interviews." A statement beneath the picture of the sheriff reads, " Sheriff Roy
Thomas of Grundy County . . . said the school and its affiliated
unions control the county's politics." In the article accompanying
the picture, Burns writes:

> I asked the sheriff if he had communistic ideas.
> " What do you mean? " he asked.
> " Well," I said, " isn't the school and its affiliated units
> considered a bit on the red side? " He made no comment.
> " The sheriff chatted a while longer with us . . . "

An affidavit made by the sheriff states:

> . . . that he has never met or spoken with a man named
> John McDougal Burns or John McDougal; and that the
> accounts of a conversation between himself and Burns,
> Published in the *Nashville Tennessean* of October 17, 1939,
> are completely false.

Other interviews were also faked in their entirety but Burns
endeavored, when convenient, to ask the person being inter-
viewed an unimportant question or two. While the subjects thus

65

briefly discussed were not used in the articles they no doubt suggested the pages of direct quotations fabricated for the public. That Burns has originality cannot be questioned.

Burns subjects his integrity as a reporter to question not only by manufacturing and elaborating interviews, but by changing the wording and meaning of a printed statement. As a member of a Committee of the Society for Curriculum Study, I wrote a chapter for *The Community School*, (D. Appleton Century, New York, 1938). An outline of a course for senior high school students on democracy read in part:

> "Social theories such as socialism, communism, and fascism would be discussed freely. Countries where these theories are being tried would be examined in the light of democratic ideals." (p. 291)

Burns quoted:

> Social theories such as . . . communism . . . should be discussed freely. Countries where *this theory* is being tried . . . should be examined in the light of our democratic ideals. (emphasis ours)

Evidently from this misrepresentation he concocts the following amazing statement which is attributed to me:

> Everyone realizes that capitalism is a failure and that we should examine communism. That is the best solution for our problem that has been offered so far.

No more need be said regarding Burns' methods. By prostituting himself for a byline he has forfeited the right to be called a reporter.

The articles raised two important questions. What is meant by " communism " and what is back of an attack on a labor school known to be identified with many progressive causes? The editorial already referred to helps us with the first question: " The fact that communism is exerting its influence in Grundy County politics is interesting. . . . "

Here is something definite. What has happened in Grundy

County politics that is attributed to the influence of communism?
Only two things of a political nature have taken place since the
Highlander Folk School was founded in 1932. Following the
reorganization of the miners and growth of unions among the
timber and WPA workers, Labor's Political Conference was organized. By agreeing on candidates to be supported in the
Democratic primary of 1938, union men were elected to the most
important county offices. The Political Conference later affiliated
with Labor's Non-Partisan League and became the first county
unit of the League in the state. The League endorsed and helped
elect the Honorable Estes Kefauver to Congress.

The other political event was the poll-tax case backed by the
Southern Conference for Human Welfare in behalf of Henry
Pirtle, a Grundy County resident. Could it be that the efforts of
working people to exercise their democratic rights is what the
Tennessean has in mind when speaking of Communism?

An editorial in the *Nashville Times*, October 26th, throws
considerable light on the second problem raised by the exposé:

> Well, well, well!
>
> So our esteemed contemporary in Nashville journalism has
> decided that the best way to start a Garner-for-President
> boom is to go awitchhunting in the Tennessee mountains.
>
> From the start, we could not understand why a city news-
> paper in Tennessee's capital would permit itself to become
> involved in a wrangle with a small labor college whose in-
> fluence hardly touches the Nashville area. . . .
>
> · · ·
>
> However, the mild-mannered, suave young secretary of the
> Highlander Folk School, who covered the state last week
> with manifestoes, affidavits, rebuttals, and replies, seems to
> have drawn blood. He guessed that a Garner-for-Presi-
> dent boom was being started in a sad, strange, way. And
> what an excitement that did cause among the mighty! . . .
>
> · · ·
>
> We had planned to ignore all this commotion until the
> Garner-for-President movement entered the picture.

67

There must be something to it, or our contemporary would not protest so much. And such a method of starting a presidential boom is too exotic to be overlooked.

William Buttrick, secretary of the Highlander Folk School, had written:

> We offer the suggestion that this may be the opening gun in the campaign to secure southern Democratic votes for John Garner in 1940.
> We understand that the *Tennessean*'s publisher is a friend and an old political associate of Mr. Garner. Now if Garner is to win, the labor movement's opposition must be overcome, particularly that of the CIO. . . .
> Perhaps Burns' articles, then, should have been entitled, " Garner for President; or how to put Cactus Jack in the White House."

The *Tennessean* replied to Buttrick in an editorial on October the 24th:

> It is true that the publisher of the *Tennessean* is a personal friend and admirer of Vice President Garner, with whom he has been associated for many years both in Texas and in Washington.

When Garner announced his candidacy for President, a December 17th editorial stated: . . . No aspirant for the highest honor in the land will better represent the popular concept of real Americanism.

Publisher Evans, an associate of Garner's in Texas, purchased the Nashville *Tennessean* in 1937 with a loan from the Reconstruction Finance Corporation headed by Jesse Jones. John McDougal Burns, who boasts of his acquaintance with Martin Dies, is also a Texan. Special releases from the Dies Committee based on charges against the school made by John P. Frey, American Federation of Labor dignitary, were provided to accompany the articles. These " specials " came from the *Tennessean*'s Washington correspondent, B. N. Rimmous, who represents a number of Texas newspapers at the capitol.

My only comment on Burns' articles, of which the first is as good a sample as any, is that Dillard King, in a sworn affidavit which has never been contested, has categorically denied that he ever said the things he was quoted as saying. The part that really ravishes me in what follows is about Dillard, a country boy who probably never saw a real live show except off the back of a medicine man's wagon, waxing sophisticated about Clifford Odets' politics. But that's how it goes on the back roads of Tennessee. All you city folks would never have dreamed that, would you?

USING GRUNDY COUNTY AS LABORATORY, SCHOOL SPREADS COMMUNIST DOCTRINES IN STATE

This is the first of the series of stories to give the inside picture of the operations of the Highlander School, written after a ten-day visit of a *Tennessean* reporter to the school and Grundy County.

By John McDougal Burns

PURPOSE AND PROGRAM

Purpose of the Highlander Folk School is to promote the progressive labor movement in the South.

The six-weeks terms for resident students are only a part of the school's program, which includes year-round community and extension activities. Staff members keep busy doing the practical work of organizing labor groups in nearby areas and carrying on educational and recreational work for the unions. Conferences and institutes are held at the school between resident periods.

OPERATES NURSERY

" Highlander operates a nursery school and conducts an educational and cultural program for the community. Music lessons are given for the young people. A library of four thousand volumes is open throughout the year."

Thus is stated in very simple, clear terms the reason for being of one of Tennessee's youngest educational institutions. But if one takes the time, as I have done, to study this "Program and Purpose" at first hand, he finds that the program is a good deal more ambitious than it appears to be, and that the purpose runs much deeper than the words indicate.

I found that Highlander Folk School, located near Monteagle in Grundy County, Tennessee, has done and is doing some rather remarkable things for such a modest institution.

This small group of "liberal" people, housed in a modest frame building a few miles from one of the state's most famous summer resorts, has not made much noise but it has achieved much. Two weeks of research, including eleven days actually spent at the school and the immediate neighborhood, have led me to the following conclusions:

CENTER FOR 13 STATES

1. It is a center, if not the center, for the spreading of Communist doctrine in thirteen Southern states.

2. Connected with its leadership are persons who have either been charged with being Communists or who have been linked definitely with Moscow.

3. Its faculty spreads Communism, approves this red doctrine, and sends its alumni into labor organizations, mostly in the South, where they maintain contact with their alma mater and spread its teachings over a wide area.

HOLDS CONFERENCES

4. It holds conferences and institutes at the school between regular sessions with its teachers expounding their Communist theories to labor leaders and others.

5. It has not restricted activities to its campus but has made an entire county (Grundy) its laboratory. Of 9,717 residents in Grundy, 1,120 have been receiving some work relief. Among these it has organized units of the Workers Alliance, concerning which, testimony before a WPA investigating committee of Congress declared the Alliance was of Communist origin. Directing this group, the school has staged strikes, elected the county sheriff and now intends to gain control of the county school system.

LEFTISTS IN GROUP

6. The school is "recognized" by state Communist headquarters in Nashville and among its guests has numbered many leftists of national reputation including Clifford Odets, the playwright, and Anna Louise Strong, editor of the Moscow Daily News in Soviet Russia for several years and who is now an author.

7. Highlander has kept in close contact with Commonwealth College, Mena, Arkansas, which is widely known for its communistic teachings and life. Often students at Highlander have attended Mena and one member of the Highlander faculty is a former professor of economics at Commonwealth.

8. The school makes available to the residents of the county, as well as to students and alumni, its library, which is well stocked with communist literature and history. The communist official organ, *The Daily Worker,* is its most popular paper.

9. It is the source of plays for use by "progressive labor" groups. The plays include communist propaganda.

10. The school, with its controlled county of Grundy, serves as a clinic for labor problems, giving instructions on strike methods, etc., but not overlooking these further opportunities to spread the leftist doctrine.

MANY QUERIES RECEIVED

For a long while the *Tennessean* has been receiving queries concerning this school. Readers, most of them residents of that area, have urged that the true status of the school be made known. So it was decided that I should go there, live at the school, and make what investigation of the situation I could.

It was decided that I should not go in the guise of a reporter, but to become an interested visitor for the duration of my visit. I dropped my surname and went under the name of John McDougal.

I went from Nashville to Chattanooga, left my car there and hitchhiked back to Monteagle. I reached the summer resort late on a Sunday night and decided that I might as well walk on out to the school which I had been informed was about two miles from town.

I had never been in Grundy County before and frankly I

didn't think the assignment was so "hot." I wondered about the type of people that I would encounter. I had heard that these mountaineers were on the taciturn side and doubted if they knew enough about communism, the capitalistic system and Moscow to answer my questions.

They'll probably think I am crazy, I decided. They won't be caring about such things, anyway.

NO LONG WAIT

But fortunately I didn't have long to wait to find out.

About a mile from Monteagle I became tired and sat down beside my suitcase to rest. I had been sitting there about five minutes when I saw a man approaching. I guessed that he must live in the region because he was dressed in a pair of overalls, wore a small coat and an old slouch hat. He had a slight mustache and was rather thin. I judged him to be about six feet tall.

"Say," I said, "could you tell me the way to Highlander Folk School?"

"So you are going to the school," he said, looking me over. "I am a student there. My name is Dillard King. I'll be glad to show you the way. But what are you doing on the road at this time of night?"

King was informed that I was a schoolteacher from Texas on a leave of absence. Having heard of the school on my travels, it was only natural a visit should result.

LOTS OF INFORMATION

King proposed that we sit by the side of the road and rest a bit as we would still have another mile or so to walk to the building. In the two-hour conversation that followed I received much information on the school and what it is doing in Grundy County today.

"We've already begun to overthrow the government," King began. "We have elected a sheriff here in opposition to the capitalists."

He told me that in the 1930 census there were 9,717 persons in the county. Of this number, he continued, 2,200 are certified for relief. He said that there were approximately 600 other wage earners in the county.

"The coal mines have played out. We are dependent upon the WPA in the main part. But we have had trouble with them and it is only through our Workers Alliance units sponsored by the Highlander Folk School that we are able to keep things running smoothly in the county," King said.

HOW ABOUT COMMUNISTS

"Well," I ventured after he had talked for some time about conditions, "how is the Communist Party in the county?"

"We've had a good chapter on and off up here for some years," King replied. "Ted Wellman down in Nashville is state secretary and comes up here pretty often. He is a good friend of the teachers over at the Highlander Folk School.

"I have visited him at his office in the Exchange Building in Nashville with Myles Horton. Myles is in charge of the school now. He's the one you will have to see if you are going to stay at the school."

My next inquiry was regarding propects of getting work at Highlander. King dispelled any hopes that I might have on that score, pointing out there was no work to be had.

"Even the unions who send students here have to pay their tuition and board," he explained. He added that finances of the school, since they were entirely based upon gifts, were low at the present time.

King referred again to the "overthrow of the government of Grundy County by the election of the sheriff."

"That shows what people as a whole think of Communism," he said. "The general public believes the Communist is a person standing with bomb in hand, ready to commit some sabotage. The way we overthrew the local government here is more in the Communistic way.

BOMBS OUT OF ORDER

"Communists are not tossing bombs now. They realize that that sort of thing is out for the present, at least," he continued.

I asked if he were a Communist.

"I didn't get to the last meeting," was his reply. "It was held about a month ago and I was sick at the time."

I asked King what he did for a living.

" I used to be on WPA and I was an organizer for the Workers Alliance for several years, then I got sick," he replied. " I hope to get back on WPA soon."

He told me that he had a wife and five children; that he eked out what salary he received from the WPA with the produce from a five-acre Grundy County farm.

" However," he said, " I get more out of life than most people do. I have been taking part with the Highlander Folk School for a long time now. And through the school I meet many interesting people."

AUTHOR VISITS SCHOOL

" Why, in April Clifford Odets, the author of *Waiting for Lefty* and *Golden Boy* came up to Highlander and read us the new play he will have on Broadway this year. He read until 4 o'clock in the morning and then drove on to Atlanta, I believe."

King was asked if Odets was known as a Communist.

" I believe he is noted for being on the left side," King replied. " I don't know if he is a member of the party. But I believe he has given money to help the school."

King then outlined the fight the Highlander group and the Grundy County Board of Education was having over the use of the Summerfield School house by the former group for a nursery school.

According to King, the board had objected to use of the school's vacant room by the Highlander group as a nursery school by members of the " Summerfield Community."

PREDICTS LEGISLATION

" We are going to elect a new legislative delegation and get a bill passed at the next session of the legislature to get rid of this board," he continued. " Then we are going to see that the right people are appointed."

King again turned the conversation to Communism.

" It has the same objectives as Socialism and right now it is just as peaceful," he said. " After all, a man has a right to be a Communist. There's nothing wrong with it."

I asked if the faculty of the school, as a whole, was in the party.

74

"You'll have to ask Myles and the others that question. That's their business," he said.

Later I did ask "Myles and the others" that question. The answer they gave me enabled me to gain access to the state Communist headquarters in Nashville, after I returned. But that's another story.

"Let's push on to the school," King said. "I know you are tired."

We walked on down the road. Soon we came to the school and I was admitted as a "guest student." I told the housekeeper, Isa Brandon, the same story that I told King.

"Hm," I thought, as I undressed for bed in the Highlander School guest room, "if King is typical of these mountain people, it looks like I'll find plenty on my visit here."

They dreamed things real strong in Tennessee, and they kept on dreaming them. Highlander was a radical experiment in democracy, and such an indecency could not be permitted to continue in Tennessee. The problem was how to get rid of it. There was a small difficulty in the fact that the Founding Fathers had apparently legalized such goings-on. One could only wonder about their lack of foresight. There were numerous encounters with the FBI, who guarded the boundaries of intolerance with their customary diligence. Some of them were hilarious, like the time an agent refused to pick up a cake from a hotel box because it was probably a part of some insidious plot. He didn't even check to see if it had a file in it. Some were more ominous, as the St. Louis *Post-Dispatch* reported on March 19, 1951:

TENNESSEE HILL PEOPLE RESENT ATTACKS ON HIGHLANDER SCHOOL
Myles Horton, Director, Tells of Policy for Racial
Democracy — Cites Programs to Aid Community

Monteagle, Tenn. . . . When FBI agents came snooping around the Highlander Folk School, the mountain people, neighbors and friends of the school, assembled to show their confidence in it and defend it. At a meeting of about fifty persons, representing many families of the Summerfield community in which the school is located, indignation was uttered and the will expressed to rebuke and rebuff attacks upon its loyalty.

The meeting was called by Myles Horton, director of the school, because the FBI agents had been circulating in the community, asking questions about Negro students attending it and watching the school at night, with the effect of creating suspicion that its policy of non-discrimination is Communistic and immoral.

Such an attitude was indicated when one of the agents, on being shown a statement of the school's aims and purposes, told Horton such aims and purposes would be considered Communistic by most Southern people.

Because of denial by the agents that they had been shown such a statement and that such a comment had been made, it has been decided by the Executive Council of the school that any further inquiries directed to the school by the FBI shall be reduced to writing.

It was when Horton found that people of the neighborhood were disturbed by the agents' inquiries that he sent a letter to each family inviting them to come to a meeting so they could be informed of what was going on. The letter expressed the hope that the school would continue to have their confidence.

"What strategy prompted the FBI agents," Horton wrote, " to watch the school by night, to harass neighbors with questions linking Negroes with Communism, is not clear. It has long been a matter of public record that they could catch us red-handed practicing racial democracy by a visit to the school."

It was clear, though, he wrote, what the results had been. A community that had for ten years accepted the presence of Negroes at Highlander without a protest had been instigated to question because they had been led by the agents' questions to infer that attendance of Negroes meant the presence of Communism. Years of community education, he declared, were being undermined by an appeal to race prejudice.

"We cannot treat democracy," he wrote, " like a hot potato that can't be handled until it cools off. To us democracy is an alive concept that must grow or die, and it can't be a little dead either."

The letter brought the school's neighbors in force to the meeting. Horton told the people that the meeting had been called to clear up possible misunderstanding about the program of the school.

" We want to know," he said, " if there is anything wrong with running a nursery school, taking people to the hospital, helping with the community hot lunch program, or with educating union people to demand their rights. We believe that the rights guaranteed by the Constitution should apply to people of all races and religions. We believe in and practice democracy and brotherhood. We have people of all races come to the school, Negroes, whites, Mexicans, and people from Europe and Asia. And we appreciate the fine way in which you have helped make them welcome in our community."

He also told them about experiments with year-round pasture for cattle in an effort to demonstrate what can be done on the mountain in the way of farming.

" If this kind of program," he said, " and supporting TVA and similar organizations is subversive, then Highlander is subversive, but we are not secret about it. We are proud of what we are doing and want everybody to know about it."

The red charges, Horton said, had been hurtful and had resulted in the loss of contributions. It had been necessary to close the nursery school. He appealed to the neighbors to help stop these rumors by refusing to be a party to the spreading of them.

He reminded them of the time when the school was under attack 10 years ago, Uncle Billy Thomas got out of his sick bed and came over to tell them that the Lord was on the side of the poor. "He stood here in this room," Horton said, "and said nobody was going to stop this school because it is a school for poor people, and the Bible is the history of the rich and powerful, and the Lord is always on the side of people like us."

Several of the neighbors spoke about what the school had meant to the community and declared their purpose to stand by it regardless of what was said against it. Dee King said his father always told him that you could kill the gossipers of a community by not repeating their gossip. Lies could be killed by living them down and that was what the school had always done.

Paul Christopher, Tennessee CIO Director, who had dropped in for a visit, said the community should be proud of the fact that Highlander is criticized by people who always oppose working people.

Many of the people expressed their faith in the program of the school and their loyalty to its purpose.

May Justus of Tracy City, Tennessee, one of the sponsors of the school wrote to Horton:

> "When racial democracy can be confused with Communism in the minds of the FBI agents, there is cause for alarm, it seems to me. Our community has come a long way in appreciating and understanding the policy of Highlander, its principles, its practice of real democracy. But this faith, fostered for so many years by living proof and example, cannot fail to suffer from the shock of a visit from the FBI in which the school's policy of nondiscrimination is given a red tag and label."

The day following the community meeting, May Justus said: "It pleased me to see so many of our neighbors at the Highlander meeting last night. It pleased me more to hear so many of them express their faith in the program of the school and their loyalty to its purpose. Certainly their sentiments were a sincere token of the people's pride in having Highlander in our community. As I walked home with a group of neighbors, some spoke to me of their hope that we could have such meetings more often. I should say that over 90 percent of the people here are with you."

This was standard procedure. The organized forces of righteousness didn't like Highlander any better than Myles Horton or I like *them*. But they couldn't make the grade. Mountain people are stubborn, and the people of Grundy County liked Highlander. Why not? It was the only institution that had ever done anything for them, and in a poor county, which Grundy unquestionably was, with a residue of raped mines and deforested hills, that's important. When you're poor, it's a nice surprise to have somebody care.

But the inquisitors never slacked off. Senator Eastland, that bastion of segregated democracy, a bag of ill wind who never blew good, had Myles in for hearings in New Orleans on March 18, 1954, in one of the witch-huntings which it has now become customary for the Congress to arrogate to itself. Before he was unceremoniously removed from these august proceedings, Myles committed a written document which is worthy of your attention:

I shall be glad to answer any questions the Committee may see fit to ask me concerning myself, for in everything I have done I have acted openly. It is not my nature to try to conceal my acts or my beliefs.

I recognize that the provisions of the Fifth Amendment of our Constitution, which provides that no person shall be required in any criminal case to be a witness against himself, is a valuable and sacred American right. This provision arose out of the lessons taught by the Inquisitions and the heresy trials, when Catholics prosecuted Protestants and Protestants prosecuted Catholics and our over-zealous forebears in Massachusetts cut off the ears of Quakers, banished Roger Williams and sent many honest men and women to the gallows as witches. This provision was designed to protect the innocent and not the guilty, and as I understand it, our law provides that no implication of guilt whatsoever shall be raised on account of its invocation. I believe that it was designed to protect people from inquisitorial proceedings such as these now being conducted by this very committee.

But, nevertheless, I do not intend to invoke the Fifth Amendment. I am fully aware that under the deteriorating moral climate of our time the reputations and even the liberties of people are constantly endangered by professional informers who go up and down the land bearing false witness against their neighbors, but this is a risk I am willing to take.

I do not believe that anything I say about myself could possibly incriminate me in any court of law where the issues are honestly tried and the guarantees of due process are observed, nor do I believe that anything I have done would incriminate me in the court of public opinion, if all the facts are freely and honestly brought out.

There are, however, some things that I cannot and will not do. I shall not and will not engage in any discussion before this Committee with respect to my opinions on people or issues, I am not here as an expert witness holding myself out as qualified to give opinion evidence. I am here under subpoena. I have expressed my opinions and beliefs openly in the past and I shall continue to express or withhold my opinions as I see fit, and to pick and choose the occasions when I will express them. I do not recognize the right of any public official or government body to require me to express them under the threat of punishment for failure to do so.

Another thing I will not do is this. I will not talk about other people who are not here to protect themselves. These things I cannot do and be true to myself. I believe the provisions of the Constitution of the United States protects me in the position that I have taken and, except for the provisions against self incrimination, I invoke them all including but not limited to:

The First Amendment, guaranteeing freedom of speech and conscience and of assembly which I believe grants freedom to remain silent under certain circumstances, as well as the freedom to speak out; the guarantees of due process set out in the Fifth Amendment; the guarantees of a fair trial before an impartial court, the right of an accused to be informed of the nature and cause of any accusations against him; to be confronted by witnesses against him and to have compulsory process for obtaining witnesses in his favor, all of which are guaranteed to American citizens by the Sixth Amendment; the provisions of the Ninth Amendment which provides that the enumeration in the Constitution of certain rights shall not be construed to deny or disparage others retained by the people as a gift of Almighty God himself, and the provisions of the Tenth Amendment which provides that powers not delegated to the U.S. by the Constitution, nor prohibited by it to the States, are reserved to the States respectively, or to the people.

I believe that our Constitution protects me. If it does not then the only Court of final resort is my own conscience and I must be bound by its decisions.

Congress has no authority to legislate concerning the opinion or beliefs of private citizens, and since this Committee derives its authority from the legislative powers of Congress, this Committee has no authority to inquire into the opinions and beliefs of private citizens. What I think and believe are my personal affairs.

The authority of this Committee is limited not only by the Constitutional limits on the powers of Congress, but also by the terms of the resolution creating this Committee. Under that resolution the Committee is charged to study the operation of laws relating to espionage and sabotage, the protection of the internal security of our country, and the effect of "subversive activity" in our country.

If I had known of any acts of espionage or sabotage or any acts which threatened our national security, I would have immediately reported them to the proper authorities for action under our laws.

The words "threat to the internal security of the United States" and "subversive activity" have become so vague, indefinite and uncertain in meaning that it is possible for them to mean different things to different men. I know that within any intelligent definition of these words, nothing that I have ever done could possibly be viewed as dangerous to the security of my country or as a subversive activity, except by the most distorted of minds.

I have acted upon the Christian postulation that all men are brothers and love freedom and that a democratic society is the only way of achieving freedom and brotherhood. These things I have taught, advocated and lived will continue to teach.

Because of my belief, I have publicly stated my opposition to your Committee and to the Committees headed by Senator McCarthy and Representative Velde. Under the guise of fighting Communism, these committees are using undemocratic methods.

Speaking as a teacher, I say that these inquisitions have damaged this country of ours by instilling fear in the teachers. A fear-ridden teacher is a poor teacher for children of free people;

and to weaken our schools is a great and obvious disservice to the cause of democracy.

The hysteria spread by your Committee and others like it has substantially contributed to the fiction that the only dynamic force in the world is Communism. This I deny. Communism has never tempted me because I believe in democracy, a powerful concept worthy of mankind the world over. You know, if you have made any effort to find out, that I have never been a member of the Communist party.

I have unshakable faith that our democratic principles (and many of them originated with Southerners like Jefferson and Mason) can demonstrate their superiority in the world market-place of ideas. I accept the challenge of Communism. It is only little and fearful men who allow their actions to be determined by fear of Communism. Back in the mountains of Tennessee where I come from, men don't scare easy.

I am fearful only of the results of our own timidity in advancing democratic principles. They should be spread now to all human relationships, from the smallest community organization to the international structures and through every social, economic and political activity. By broadening the scope of democracy to include everyone, and deepening the concept to include every relationship, the hosts of democracy would be so vast and so determined that nothing evil could stand in their path.

De-segregation and integration of the public schools for example, would spectacularly refresh the democratic thesis everywhere. The inspiration of such an event would reach into the remotest corners of Asia, and Africa — and Mississippi and truly would be heard " round the world."

For lack of any evident reason, I am compelled to ask whether it is because I have expressed these views and have acted on these principles that I am now haled before this Committee?

I suppose that in the eyes of some of the members of this Committee, opposition to segregation is " subversive." But, as an American, I am unwilling to assume that a legislative group bearing the authority of my Government represents the dark and dismal outlook that justified slavery in the dead past and which today equates the fight for the full democratic rights of all men, including Negroes, with Communism.

An honest American voice speaks here. Nobody there listened, especially not the Chairman of the Subcommittee on Internal Security of the Senate Judiciary Committee. But a lot of other people did listen, as a Highlander release a few months later demonstrated. A few sample quotes will give the flavor:

A copy of your statement has been brought to my attention and I want to congratulate you on it. We need courage in these difficult days and I feel your statement shows just that.

Mrs. Franklin D. Roosevelt

This was one of the worst cases of the caprice of Congressional Committees which we have had, and shows that McCarthyism runs far beyond McCarthy. I can only express my confidence in your integrity and my regret that you have been subjected to this kind of treatment.

Reinhold Niebuhr
Union Theological Seminary, New York

I want you to know that I think you raised the significant question when you asked at New Orleans if a good American could not make a statement. I was proud to read about the way you conducted yourself.

Harold Wiley Freer, minister
Dover Congregational Church
Westlake, Ohio

That's a good statement you got out, and needed. You took just the right position for a courageous and self-respecting citizen in these timid days. What a scandalous performance a senator can put on when he plays cops and robbers!

Roger Baldwin, New York

I thought you handled yourself with great dignity and honesty.
Theodore Brameld, New York University

To me, the most interesting thing about the whole procedure was the fact that the *Montgomery Advertiser* took and published a poll of nine newspaper correspondents, which I am sure you saw, in which four said that Senator Eastland, among the principals, represented the greatest threat to American liberty; one thought the committee counsel, Aron, deserved the honor, and two voted for your friend Crouch. (What a character and what a name!)

James P. Warburg, New York

It seems to me that the public is at last waking up to the evil nature of many of the methods used by the Congressional investigating committees. I believe therefore that you may look forward to the future without untoward anticipations. More power to you!

Douglas Horton, minister
The Congregational Christian Churches
New York

So what happened? The attacks continued, in infinite and dreary unvariety including a few we shall consider later for other reasons, but the real show got on the road in 1958. It was instigated by that well-known Tennessean, Governor Griffin of Georgia, a staunch believer in States Rights and a friend of good democrats everywhere. White ones, that is, who can be trusted to vote the straight party line in Georgia. Myles Horton obviously couldn't be, which radically altered the two-party system in Georgia, where, as a Tennessean, he was undemocratically deprived of a vote. Strong measures were clearly called for, especially since nobody, in all the investigations, had ever been able to pin anything on Highlander. The place was getting too successful, and already they were beginning to sing "We Shall Overcome" all over the South. Well really, you know. And after all.

You have to have grown up in the South to realize how much talk there is about States Rights and what a crock of malarkey it usually is. There's nothing handier when you want to get your own way.

So we talk States Rights until we need to gang up on

somebody. Then we get together as a bloc. As has happened in every election in modern history, as the apologists for this dogma seldom get around to pointing out. The Solid South is built on fear, and whether it goes against Al Smith or for Goldwater, it does it by disfranchising most of its population. We act as a bloc, and when a place like Highlander, which had committed the sin of actually practicing the democracy all Southern Congressmen preach at chicken dinners and barbecues, gets to be a threat to Southern Purity, in John Edgerton's classic phrase, it's time for concerted action.

So the boys ganged up on Highlander. It's as simple as that.

The happy occasion was a celebration. It was Highlander's twenty-fifth anniversary, and 179 participants, most of them distinguished, gathered for a Labor Day seminar. By that September weekend of 1957 even the Supreme Court had gotten around to admitting that integration was here to stay, arrogating unto itself, " wholly without authority," as Governor Griffin had sagely remarked a year before, " the right to change the law of the land." The fact that this is precisely the Court's legal responsibility, its sole function under the doctrine of the separation of powers, another thing these boys like to bleat about on Sunday if there are enough voters around, apparently escaped the Governor's keen legal mind. As did such a minor point as the fact that the only " law of the land " related to segregation was a prior construction of the Fourteenth amendment by the same High Court which had sanctified the doctrine of " separate but equal."

But don't let the inconsistency bother you. When you're dealing with these boys it's wise to hold on to your hat, cross everything you've got two of, and pray for rain.

One of the distinguished guests was Martin Luther King, Jr., not then the anathema for white racists he later became — as usual, Highlander was running way ahead of Supreme Courts and Nobel Prize Committees and not even breathing hard — but nevertheless a preacher who, uncharacteristically for his trade, had stuck his neck out during the Montgomery bus boycott and was one of the founders of the newly formed Southern Christian Leadership Conference. Less distinguished were two strangers who, in the manner of John McDougal Burns, wandered in under false pretenses. One of these was Ed Friend, then serving on special assignment for Governor Griffin's Georgia Commission on Education.

Friend represented himself as an employee of another department of the State of Georgia — a position which he had formerly held and to which he subsequently returned, when the dirty work was done — and as an amateur photographer who liked to pick up a little money on the side doing free-lance work. He just happened to be passing through and thought he might take some pictures of this momentous occasion. Myles, being too busy with important things to think like a public relations man, had neglected to lay in a photographer. It seemed like a good idea, and a deal was made.

Also present, by an interesting coincidence, was one other stranger, a Negro staff writer for the *Daily Worker* named Abner Berry. He passed himself off as a free-lance writer who had always admired Highlander and would like to take some notes for a possible article on the school. He neglected to mention his connection with the *Daily Worker*. It would have been all right that he was, but he would then have been identified and introduced in his true capacity, as were other newsmen present.

86

To understand this slimy little story you need to remember that the other participants were invited guests. Highlander's tradition has always been that there is room at the inn, but this was an important occasion, a celebration of the improbable fact that the school had endured for twenty-five years, and it had been carefully planned. But since it has always been a school with nothing to hide, Berry and his Friend — I couldn't resist that one — were welcomed. Two more didn't matter that much.

Interesting coincidences developed. Nobody else knew Berry or Friend, but they seemed to know each other. When Myles observed this, they told him that they had been discussing their mutual interest in free-lance work and that Berry could perhaps use some of Friend's pictures in his article. At the time, that seemed to make sense.

But it began to be clear that every time Friend took a picture Berry just happened to be around to be in it. As an undistinguished casual guest at a conference attended by a lot of important people, he might have been expected, in simple decency, to hang back while other people were being photographed. Unfortunately, there was no decency involved in this shabby con game. Friend usually managed to fiddle around until Berry got on the scene.

This reached a climax in the picture that became a feature of a glossy sheet about Highlander which Governor Griffin used funds presumably intended for education to distribute by the hundreds of thousands. It was a posed picture with Myles, Aubrey Williams, and Martin Luther King, among others, in the front row. It was intended to be a part of the historical record of the conference, but Friend needed to have his fink in the picture to hang the Communist tag on the meeting, so at the last minute he had Berry scuttle down

the aisle and squat like a dog with the trots in *front* of the front row.

Myles got mad. Not because he yet understood the game they were playing, but because he was sick of having Berry, for what he then assumed were reasons of personal publicity-seeking, horn in where he wasn't supposed to be.

" I won't pay for that picture," he said to Friend.

He didn't, either, and believe me, he didn't need to. Martin Luther King is identified here only as " of the Montgomery Boycott," but when they finally realized how tough an opponent he was, the picture was escalated into the notorious billboard labeled " Martin Luther King at Communist Training School." The only consolation is the irony of these know-nothings still trying to hang the Communist label on the nonviolent winner of the Nobel Peace Prize. Of course that's awarded by the King of Sweden, and you know how those foreigners are. The things they do. On unsegregated beaches and in broad daylight yet. If the racists only knew enough history to realize that Old Alfred Nobel invented dynamite, maybe they'd feel better about the whole thing. That's the kind of language they understand, and I offer them the information for free. Unfortunately, they settled for a rifle instead.

There are two other pictures in that flyer which are worth noting. One is important only for its caption. It's a muddy group-shot labeled as follows: " Rosa Parks, who precipitated the Montgomery, Alabama, Bus Boycott, and Ralph Tefertiller of New York's Henry Street Settlement listen to group under the watchful eye of Abner Berry of the Central Committee of the Communist Party. Berry reported the meeting of this Communist Training School in his column in the *Daily Worker* of September 10, 1957." Berry is there all right, in another posed position *apart* from the group. I will

say that for a mastermind he didn't relate very well. Maybe he needed a little more private ingroup training from the Georgia Commission on Education.

The other picture was the *pièce de résistance*, a picture of a happy middle-aged white woman, a country schoolteacher type, who appeared to be embracing a young Negro. A good idea too, I say, only that isn't what happened. They were doing an old folk dance where the partners put their arms around each other and clap their hands, as any honest man looking at the picture can plainly see. But the picture, which radiates simple joy, was neither taken nor distributed by honest men.

Before I give you, if you have a strong stomach, some insight into the minds of the people involved here, I'd like to make a personal statement. This is an angry book, as you may have noted at a point or two along the way, but it's not an unfair one. I'm angry because I'm a white Southern Protestant and proud to be. It's my heritage. I'm also proud that racial prejudice never made any sense to me. I never thought it made you any worse to be colored, and I never thought it made you any better either. I don't care about anything except what's inside a man, and it's my sad report, after fifty years, that there aren't enough good ones, of whatever variety, to go around.

I don't feel any blood guilt. For my money, that's a myth Faulkner might better have abandoned back in Yoknapatawpha County. It helped him get off the hook, but I don't feel any need to get off a hook I was never personally on. I feel a responsibility to do something about the treatment of the Negro and all other minorities — including writers like me — in America, but that's just because I believe in humanity. We humans are a pretty sad lot, usually, but we're all we've got to go on. Though I'm going to have to deal with racism, black and white, before we're through, it's not a subject that really interests me. It is only a problem that has to be faced.

But about the South I feel something different. All Southerners, black or white, are my people in a way nobody else in the world is except my marvelous Slovak wife who happens to share our Southern brand of primitivism. That primitivism, like nationalism anywhere, is our curse and our virtue. It's made us the most violent region in America; it's also made us the most creative. I wouldn't be the kind of writer I am if I had been born and raised anywhere else. It's a writer's country, even though most of us never read a book. For some people Chicago is Home and Heaven; for others it's the Bronx. For some it's California, but the percentage of natives is so rare there you can forget it. I've spent a lot of my life around all these places, but for me Home never really starts north of the Mason-Dixon line.

Therefore I violently resent the impudence of men like those I've been describing in presuming to talk for my people. They've managed to make themselves sound like the majority, but they're not. They represent everything worst about us, and they sell their particular line of garbage because it appeals to the provincialism which is also a part of our inheritance. Myles Horton speaks for the real South, and I like to think I do too. Myles stayed home and created a world in action which represents the best part of our traditions. I went away and tried to do the same thing in books. But we've both been fighting the same fight.

I want to say, in a preliminary way, just what I think that tradition is. The primary message of this book, which will not please most radicals, Northern or Southern, black or white, is that the South is the last and perhaps only place where our society has any real hope. The reason is very sim-

ple. Much as we've made a mess of it, this is the only part
of the country where two races have made any progress in
working together on things important to them both. They
were very simple things and the reasons were mostly economic, but they worked.

What I emphatically don't mean is the standard Southern
liberal rationalization that they "understand" Negroes. One
of the things you can depend on about any liberal is that he
doesn't understand much but can talk up a storm about it.
Most of this fancy talk has regularly been devoted to justify-
ing the intolerable suppression the white man has exercised
on the black. But the talkers don't matter. It's the country
people, black and white, working together because they have
to depend on each other, who are our hope.

Many of Highlander's eminent supporters never really understood what Myles Horton was up to, much as they admired his work. Governor Griffin understood it all right because it hurt him where he lived. He used the Communist
label because that's the kind of convenient tag his kind likes
to hand out, but that wasn't what worried him and everybody knew it. Myles has been much more of a threat to the
parasites of the established order, of whom the good Governor is a prime example, than any Communist. Communism never really made any headway in the South, despite
some good and brave work by individual labor organizers in
the thirties, because the party never understood the things
I've just been saying. It never can or will get anywhere in
America because such a monolithic organization can't cope
with pluralism, which is democracy, which is diversity, which
is our only hope. When our police state arrives it will be
homegrown.

The kind of diversity the Governor and his cronies
couldn't face was integration. All Myles was doing in that

little old school in Tennessee was getting people together to try to help them learn how to cope with their own programs. He never made any bones about it, including the fact that he didn't give a damn what color the students were. The real threat to a political system that survives on cultivating the prejudices of a minority of the population comes when people start to put their heads together and figure out what's best for *them*. That's been the radical thing about Highlander, and that's why they had to try to get it.

They did too, or so they thought, but it took some doing. And of course all they really accomplished was to make Highlander more secure than ever. What the know-nothings never realize is that you can't smear a good idea out of existence and that the best publicity you can give it is irresponsible attacks. One of the most consoling facts I know is that in the year after the Tennessee Courts finally managed to padlock Highlander, its income from contributions — Highlander's, that is, not the State's — *doubled*. There's a good one to think over on a dark day.

But this was in the future. Meanwhile, while Governor Griffin's dogs were gnawing their dry bones, more responsible organizations, to commit the understatement of this page, were reporting the conference somewhat differently. The St. Louis *Post Dispatch* will serve as a model:

ON A TENNESSEE MOUNTAIN TOP

Last week marked the start of the second quarter century of the Highlander Folk School atop the Cumberland mountain range, near Monteagle, Tenn. Some two hundred people of diverse racial and religious strains from all over the South gathered at the residential adult school to celebrate the occasion by taking part in a seminar on "The South Thinking Ahead."

In the twenty-five years that are now Highlander history, there were times when Myles and Zilphia Horton must have wondered whether their experiment in teaching people to live and work together would survive. But it did and one of Highlander's neighbors, Miss May Justus, told why:

As the years went by it was clearly seen that the school's purpose was to improve the living condition of the people on the mountain. Zilphia Horton more than anyone else trained the children and with her musical talent made glad the hearts of young and old alike. Highlander opened its doors and made possible the one and only place for recreation for the community of Summerfield. A weekly paper, a nursery school and a film center are among the many activities that helped the people of the local community.

Now Highlander's community is much larger than the mountain top around Monteagle. It is so large that it drew to the seminar Dean John B. Thompson of the University of Chicago, Bishop D. Ward Nichols of Jacksonville, Florida, the Rev. Martin Luther King and Aubrey Williams, both of Montgomery, Alabama, Alonzo Moron, president of Hampton Institute, and many other group leaders.

The Highlander school is helping remake the South. It has done a lot in its quiet, modest way. It has much to do. May its second quarter century see the fulfillment of the goals of freedom and justice that guide its modern pioneers.

The Georgia smear sheet broke three months later, previously heralded by inside stories about its portentousness. It labeled the Labor Day celebration a Communist Training School set up to discuss methods and tactics of precipitating racial strife and disturbance. Ignoring the fact that racial strife had been precipitated long since by people of their own stripe and that Highlander's purpose was to find a solution for it, the Griffin boys made the customary identification of integration with Communism. The usual tactics of guilt by association were freely employed, including the standard assumption that anyone accused before such worthies as Senator Eastland by professional ex-Communists like Paul Crouch was automatically guilty. Abner Berry's anonymous, dishonest, and curiously coincidental appearance was described as "insuring the Communist Party against deviations from the Party principle."

No question, it's an educational document. "It behooves each of us," says an editorial signed by the Governor, "to learn more of Communist infiltration and the direction of Communist movements. Only through information and knowledge can we combat this alien menace to Constitutional government." Accurate information, that is, like this glossy smear of a group of dedicated and distinguished people, including aliens like Myles Horton.

Highlander's response was as dignified as this attack was slanderous. They issued the following statement, signed by Reinhold Niebuhr, Lloyd K. Garrison, Monsignor John O'Grady, and Eleanor Roosevelt.

Governor Marvin Griffin of Georgia has adopted the dangerous technique of charging all Southern integration leaders with being Communist inspired.

We refer to a four-page, banner-headlined, slick paper publication, a quarter of a million copies of which are now being distributed bearing the imprint of the Georgia Commission on Education. This body, whose chairman is Governor Griffin of Georgia, was created by the legislature of that state in 1935 for the purpose of uncovering ". . . a master plan, Soviet inspired, behind the racial incidents so widespread in America today." In this year of 1957, four years after its creation, the Commission has apparently decided it can best serve its purpose by the issuance of a document proclaiming the discovery that a widely advertised seminar conducted over the 1957 Labor Day weekend at the Highlander Folk School in Monteagle, Tennessee, constituted a "Communist Training School" in the tactics of racial strife. The Commission said: "During Labor Day Weekend, 1957, there assembled at Highlander the leaders of every major race incident in the South, prior to that time since the Supreme Court decision." (sic)

The seminar attacked by Governor Griffin was one of a series of workshops, each from one to six weeks in duration, held by Highlander since 1953 to develop plans and leaders for an orderly, peaceful transition from segregated to integrated schools.

Highlander Folk School, chartered in 1932, is a resident center for adult education, located on the Cumberland Mountain in Tennessee. Here adult students come together the year round from all walks of life without reference to color, religion, schooling or economic status to study and to discuss challenging social, educational and economic problems confronting individuals and communities in the South.

Among those attending the seminar in question were: Dr. Alonzo G. Moron, President of Hampton Institute; Dean Charles Gomillion, Dean of Students of Tuskegee; Rev. David H. Brooks, Tallahassee; Rev. Martin Luther King and Rev. Ralph Abernathy of Montgomery, Alabama, and Professor John Hope II of Fisk University. Some of the subjects under discussion were the implications of integration for such groups as churches, schools and trade unions.

In replying to the charges of Governor Griffin, Myles Horton, Director and Founder of Highlander, stated: "Highlander takes pride and assumes full responsibility for the speakers and discussion leaders. Highlander did not and does not welcome enrollment of anyone with a totalitarian philosophy whether from the extreme right or from the extreme left. In these troubled times, nothing but more trouble can come from the White Citizens Councils and the Communist Party's infiltration into groups earnestly seeking a democratic solution to our problems. Both are morally bankrupt and have nothing to offer. We want only those at Highlander who do their own thinking."

The attempt of the Georgia Governor's Commission to draw from the serious and fruitful deliberations of this gathering sustenance for the efforts of the Southern racists to equate desegregation with communism evokes our strong condemnation. This kind of irresponsible demagoguery is obviously designed to intensify the difficulties confronting decent Southerners who might otherwise give leadership in the adjustment necessary for the desegregation which is inevitable. We deem it morally indefensible for any man or group to inflict upon such institutions as Highlander and upon such individuals as the respected leaders, both white and Negro, who attended the Labor Day Seminar, the damage to reputation and position which may result from the wide distribution of this slanderous material.

Dr. John Dewey was, until his death, the chairman of the Highlander Committee of Sponsors. He said, "I regard Highlander Folk School as one of the most important social-educational projects in America."

Malcolm S. Knowles, Executive Director of The Adult Education Association of the United States, says, ". . . Highlander stands out as a beacon in the pioneering of a new institutional form, the residential adult school . . . I would place Highlander high on any list of adult educational institutions including universities, public schools, libraries, and private social agencies."

We hope that the vast majority of Americans irrespective of geographical location will join us rather than Governor Griffin in subscribing to the principles set forth in Highlander's official statement of policy:

> "Democracy to us means that membership in the human family entitles all to freedom of thought and religion, to equal rights to a livelihood, education and health; to equal opportunity to participate in the cultural life of the community and to equal access to public facilities.
>
> "With a democratic goal, we are in a position to fight anything that gets in the way, whether it be totalitarian communism, or fascism. . . . "

The statement was later signed by many others, all distinguished, but that's unimportant. What does matter is that this is said with simplicity and eloquence. Let's compare the deep thoughts of Governor Griffin:

It was only in 1954 that the Supreme Court of the U.S. wholly without authority arrogated unto itself the right to change the law of the land.

For the nine men who sit upon the Supreme Court to usurp

these powers which do not belong to them but which belong exclusively to Congress and to the states is a monumental fall which is shocking, outrageous, and reprehensive. Such fraudulent conduct, my friends, imposes no obligations upon the states to acquiesce or upon the people to bow their necks to this new form of tyranny.

Let me say to you tonight as we counsel together, do not be concerned about what is said by the communists, pinkos, radicals, NAACP, ADA, the one-worlders and all that motley group of crackpots who are clamoring for desegregation and mongrelization.

You may take a map of the world today; wherever you find a country populated by a black race, the colored race or a mongrel race, the Christian religion has not been able to survive. The white people have missionaries there now trying to keep alive a spark of the Christian religion.

The white race are the only people able to perpetuate the Christian religion.

Mongrelization of the people in America will follow school integration on the social level. It will bring with it destruction of the Christian religion. Integration will destroy both the race and religion.

Let's look also at Ed Friend, performing at the investigation by the legislature of the state of Tennessee which this smear sheet provoked. It should be remembered that he was testifying under oath:

. . . They divided the seminar up into workshops. They had one group that was called a religious group. They had another one that was called a labor group. They had another group called a social welfare group, and it seems like there were two more, but I don't recall those. The reason that I particularly remembered those, Fred Routh, from the Southern Regional Council, whose offices are in the Wesley Memorial Church Building in Atlanta, was there, and presided over that meeting in Mr. Horton's home. That was the largest gathering of them all. The one on religion was in charge of a young lady whose name I don't have, and in that group was a man by the name of Browne from

Koinonia Farms, who came up there and was telling what a horrible time they were having down in Georgia because they were trying to integrate a farm down there, and I went to that because Mr. Browne was there. That was the religious group. They went on to tell how they had to get in on any means or methods they could to get their story across to the church people so that they would help them in their integration problem.

Q. — In this religious meeting, did they ever open that with prayer or close it with prayer?

A. — No, sir, they did not.

Q. — At any time throughout the meeting did they have prayer?

A. — No, sir.

Q. — Mr. Friend, was that a subversive meeting there at that time?

A. — It was subversive, Sir, to the way that I have been taught to live in America.

Q. — Explain that to the committee.

A. — I have been taught by Southern tradition to keep the races separate. I was taught to go to Sunday School and church. I was taught to respect the other fellow's habitat, and that is what I have always tried to do. Up here it seems like all of those things weren't even considered. It is the primary motive of this group to tear down the forces that were trying to keep the races separate in the South.

Q. — Was it your observation that they were trying to bring about a condition of chaos and turmoil and strife and stress among people?

A. — Among the races, Sir, between the races.

Q. — Is it true or not that that is the breeding ground for Communists under those conditions?

A. — That is my understanding of it, Sir.

How a small-time fink like Ed Friend, an inept bureaucrat with more energy than brains, ended up testifying before a legislative investigation by the great state of Tennessee takes a little examining. The Attorney General of the state of Arkansas, Bruce Bennett by name, took the ball from Governor

Griffin and recommended to the Tennessee legislature that the Highlander Folk School be closed. "I would gladly come to Tennessee if invited," he said, "to lend any help I could." He came all right; he was expected. He and Myles Horton were the principal witnesses and the hearings ended up in the usual way: they couldn't pin anything on Highlander.

Less august institutions than the Tennessee legislature were not so pleased with the state of Arkansas's taking over local decisions. On the high policy level, as we have already noted, States Rights are a convenience which you get under the day it rains. But on a local level, it's different. You live by it. And it's what a lot of folks died for back in that disturbance now called the Civil War. In my part of the country it's still The War Between The States, and that's what the Southerners who died in it thought it was about.

So they didn't particularly cotton in Tennessee to having the state of Arkansas coming over to tell them how to run their business. Even the Nashville *Tennessean,* not a newspaper notably friendly to Highlander, had this to say:

Why Conduct a Witch Hunt for Arkansas?

In approving an investigation of the Highlander Folk School by voice vote instead of by a roll call, the state legislature indicated a certain uneasiness about this adventure.

And well it might have, for the whole thing has the appearance of a witch hunt.

This would be unfortunate in any circumstances. It is all the more so in view of the fact that the Tennessee legislature has allowed itself to be used by the attorney general of Arkansas, whose record at home is hardly a recommendation for importing his talents or ideas here.

It is not necessary to agree with the teachings of the Highlander school to deplore the spirit behind the investigation the legislature has now authorized. Its ultra-liberal philosophy has, in fact, won the school more critics than admirers.

But that is not the point. The point is that Highlander has made no attempt to hide its views or its activities. Unpopular though its philosophy may be, the school openly stands on it. And as one of the backers of the investigation said in an unguarded moment yesterday in the house, the school has received enough publicity in the last fifteen years to make everyone familiar with it.

Furthermore, the institution has been repeatedly investigated by various groups, including the un-American activities committee of the United States House of Representatives, and nothing has been turned up that wasn't already known.

What, then, does the Tennessee legislature now hope to accomplish?

Until presented to the house for action yesterday, the resolution calling for the probe did not even say. When this oversight was called to the attention of the sponsors, an amendment was adopted to provide for recommendations leading to " appropriate legislative action."

But that is so fuzzy as to be almost meaningless, and it does not answer the question of just what it is that the legislature might do after its investigating committee has completed its work.

Nor does it dispel the suspicion that the real purpose — despite the communism smoke screen — is to harass and intimidate the institution because of its candid advocacy of integration, which is the reason it does not please Atty. Gen. Bruce Bennett of Arkansas.

It is one thing to disagree with Highlander on this issue — or on any other — but it is quite another to talk of closing the school because of it, which is the course advocated by Mr. Bennett.

As thousands of youngsters in Little Rock can testify, Mr. Bennett is an expert on closing schools. But that is just one more reason Tennessee should reject his gratuitous offer of assistance in the Highlander matter.

If the day comes when minority views are not tolerated in this country, no matter how unpopular they may be, then democracy will have lost its meaning. That may be no concern to Mr. Bennett, but it should give pause to the officials and people of Tennessee before they follow the advice of this interloper any farther.

The resolution calling for the probe now goes to Governor Ellington. The courageous thing to do would be to veto it. Short of that, he should exercise extreme caution in naming the committee members so the probe can be kept in reasonable bounds.

If there is anything Tennessee does not need at this point, it is the distinction of reviving McCarthyism.

It was even more blunt a week later:

It's Just Possible They Aren't Infallible

"Where is the man," asked John Locke in his classic Essay on Human Understanding, "that has incontestable evidence of the truth of all he condemns; or can say that he has examined to the bottom all his own, or other men's opinions?"

Well, events of the last week suggest that there is one man in Tennessee and another in Arkansas who, in their own estimation at least, feel qualified to step up and answer, "Right here." And there is more of a connection between the two men than might meet the eye of a casual observer.

The Tennessean is Mr. Harry Lee Senter, a state representative from Bristol. The Arkansan is Atty. Gen. Bruce Bennett. On a single day last week, these two asserted their own infallibility by urging the suppression of ideas and opinions that differ from their own.

Ostensibly, Mr. Senter was speaking in behalf of his resolution to investigate the Highlander Folk School. But he took the occasion to make a passionate denunciation of "the left-wingers, the Communists, the do-gooders and the one-worlders" — everybody, in other words, who doesn't necessarily believe that Harry Lee Senter is always right.

And he made it plain that it was his desire to silence these dissidents by harassing them with the kind of investigation he was even then proposing. "Our central purpose," he explained "is to root out that which is evil."

Mr. Bennett was even more direct, for he submitted to the Arkansas legislature a bill that would make it unlawful for anyone to encourage *nonconformance with the established traditions, customs and usage of the state.*

This is, of course, a segregation measure. But it is one of the most extreme proposals that has yet been laid before any Southern legislature and could, if enacted, go far beyond the segregation question to strike at the very fundamentals of a free and democratic society.

It is, in essence, a thought control bill of the most vicious kind. And it assumes special significance for Tennessee because its sponsor, Mr. Bennett, is the very person who encouraged Tennessee to undertake the investigation that Mr. Senter urged to " root out that which is evil."

It is beside the point that Highlander Folk School feeds on the kind of publicity Mr. Senter, at Mr. Bennett's prodding, is giving it.

The point is that the school has a right to its opinions and ideas, however unpopular they may be. So do all other Americans, and any attempt to pour everybody into one mold and enforce a single line of thought is thoroughly alien to the democratic concept.

Strange though it may seem to the Messrs. Senter and Bennett, it is possible that they do not have a monopoly on truth. That being the case, we would call to their attention — and to the attention of any others infatuated with their own infallibility — an observation that is no less timely now than it was when John Stuart Mill made it more than a century ago:

" The peculiar evil of silencing the expression of an opinion is that it is robbing the human race; posterity as well as the existing generation; those who dissent from the opinion still more than those who hold it. If the opinion is right, they are deprived of the opportunity of exchanging truth for error; if wrong, they lose what is almost as great a benefit, the clearer perception and livelier impression of truth, produced by its collision with error."

The probe laid an egg, as usual, the investigators having never figured out, as they never do, why the chicken crosses the road. Here is the *Tennessean's* final editorial summation:

PROBE "DRAMA" LAYS AN EGG

The two-act "drama" written by Reps. Shelby Rhinehart and Harry Lee Senter and directed by Sen. Barton Dement has closed after a brief run before near-empty houses.

Entitled, "Highlander Folk School Investigation," it had some interesting casting and some dialogue in which the so-called "villains" outperformed the so-called "heroes." Despite such touches as a 12-minute movie and the appearance of a guest star from Arkansas, it left considerable to be desired as a play, comedy or drama.

As a serious investigation, for which taxpayers shelled out $5,000 — perhaps more since some of the "actors" are reported to demand extra pay beyond their $15 a day — it was pretty much the dud of the advance predictions.

The Tracy City hearing produced some backfiring queries but little else except hearsay evidence and the "belief" of many that Highlander is somehow connected with subversives. The Nashville portion brought on more backfiring of queries and became so confused that the issue of subversion finally devolved into argument about the school's charter and then into a small, technical point of law over the handling and reporting of school funds.

Arkansas Atty. Gen. Bruce Bennett's advance-publicized "blast" at Highlander was merely the replaying of some tired old sound effects heard many times in this state. All that the hot-blowing Arkansan had to contribute in the way of facts was already available to committee hands from the files of previous U.S. house and senate probes of Highlander — none of which, it must be said, ever succeeded in pinning a subversive charge on the school.

At most, the investigating committee succeeded only in stirring up the kind of controversy that Highlander thrives upon. In so doing, it detracted from the reputation of Tennessee as a fairminded and liberty-loving state which doesn't approve of witch hunts for the sake of political notice — especially for the political notice of an attorney general from Arkansas.

Similar editorials appeared, that March of 1959, in the Chattanooga *Times* and the Kingsport *Times News*. Responsible Tennesseans might, and often did, disapprove of Highlander, but they disapproved of the character of this investigation even more.

Nevertheless, the whole history of Highlander had moved into a new phase. It was now only a matter of time. The legislative committee, in recommending that Highlander's charter be revoked, issued, through Senate Joint Resolution Number 47, a mandate to the courts to find a way to do the job. Having failed so miserably themselves, they left the method up to the judicial branch. Ab Sloan, the District Attorney General for the Eighteenth Judicial Court, into whose purview the assignment fell, was not slow to find the means. He raided the school on the pretense of searching for liquor.

After the raid, Sloan was reported thus by the Nashville *Tennessean:*

The raid, which he directed, was for the purpose of finding whiskey so that he could have the school closed. He had information that liquor could be found at Highlander and decided that this route would be easier than trying to prove other allegations against the school.

" The members of the legislative committee," he said, " gave me information mostly on integration and communism, and I wasn't satisfied I could be successful at that. I thought maybe this was the best shot and I think now I'll be successful."

The quality of this gentleman's mind, to strain a phrase, is best illustrated by a brief excerpt from his later summation to the court:

The President of the Highlander Folk School, and I have got nothing against him personally, is not even a party to this lawsuit. He has never been served. It is the institution that I am after and he is president of the institution. And I don't care what they teach, be it racial integration, or be it communism or be it whatever they want it. I'm not interested in that. I'm not an educator, I am a little, measly, feeble, attorney general of this circuit trying to do the very best I can. . . . What did Mr. Carl Geary say about this thing? Have you ever heard it? I have never heard this described in such short sentences as what it is, an *integrated whorehouse*. I don't care if it is integrated or not. I am after it. It is against the law to have one of them in Grundy County and it is my duty to do what I have done and I have got no apologies to make for it. That is what it is. And under the statute, Your Honor has the power and that is why the Legislature gave it to you. If it is proven to the satisfaction of the Court this thing wants to be stopped now, not in November. That is why the Legislature gave Your Honor the power to abate it and stop it now and it is the gathering, and the meeting of these people together that creates the situation that we have heard so much proof about.

A particularly pleasing feature of this small attraction is the accuracy with which the Honorable District Attorney General was able to describe himself. It was the only piece of objectivity he displayed during the entire proceedings.

On the night of Friday, July 31, 1959, forty members of a workshop on community leadership at Highlander were enjoying the banquet which traditionally preceded the Saturday morning closing session. Dinner was over. The dishes were still on the table, including cups and glasses in which milk and coffee had been served. Those participants still in the dining room were enjoying a movie, *The Face of the South*.

At 8:40 cars began to arrive in the driveway. A man who later proved to be a deputy, though he was wearing a sportshirt and no badge, came over to two women who were talking on the lawn and flashed a light in their faces. The women, thinking they were being molested, ran toward two men, one of them Esau Jenkins, who will return in our narrative, who were also talking outside. Several others of the raiding party appeared to round up all of them, including two women seated on the steps. One of these, Bernice Robinson, broke away and called inside that there were men annoying the women.

Ordered inside, they found the room milling with armed men, in uniforms and plain clothes. One of the men said, " We want Septima Clark." Mrs. Clark, Educational Director of Highlander and acting Director during Myles Horton's absence abroad at an Adult Education Conference, a remarkable Negro woman to whom we shall return, was in the dining room operating the projector. While the visiting gentry were waiting for her, Ab Sloan, dressed in plain clothes with no indication that he held an official position, noticed Guy Carawan, a folksinger on the school staff, discussing a singing program with some young people.

" What's your name? " Sloan said roughly.

Guy is not a man who likes to be pushed around.

" Who am I talking to? " he asked.

" This man looks drunk," Sloan said. " Maybe we better take him to the car."

" Want to see what we've been drinking? " Guy said, striking a chord on his guitar.

One of the men went back to the kitchen with him, sampled the punch, and found it to be fruit juice. He returned, leaving Guy unmolested.

For the time being.

Mrs. Clark came out of the dining room and asked what they wanted.

" We have a warrant to search this house," Sloan said, " and I want you to listen while this officer reads it to you."

" What are you searching for? " Septima asked.

" Whiskey."

"Then go ahead and look," she said. "You won't find any whiskey in this house."

While the warrant was being read, a lengthy procedure since police officers and deputies are not notably fast readers, the search proceeded in the considerate fashion customary in such situations. Bedrooms were entered, coverings were ripped off beds, bureau drawers were emptied on the floor, books were pulled down and torn apart. From Mrs. Clark's room they took a wallet containing an air travel card, identification papers, and about twenty-one dollars, and, from a small metal box which they broke open, her bankbook. The office was ransacked and the kitchen thoroughly searched. The refrigerator, which was to feature largely in the subsequent trials as a repository for beer, contained nothing more intoxicating than orange pop.

A thorough search in the classic style.

But no booze.

In the dining room the movie continued, and the audience, however perplexed, watched it quietly.

After the warrant had been read, Mrs. Clark asked to call James Hargis, manager of the school property. The phone was answered by a policeman. The search was going on at Hargis' house too.

When she returned, an officer said, "You're under arrest."

"For what?"

"For possessing whiskey."

"But there's not any whiskey here."

"Never you mind. The General said so. Come on."

"Where did you find it?" Sally Freedman, another staff member, asked.

"Never mind, we have it — you'll see it later." And to Mrs. Clark, "Come on, you."

"Just let me talk to my granddaughter," Mrs. Clark said.

Her granddaughter, Yvonne, six years old and motherless, was hysterical. "Why are they taking my mama to jail?" she kept saying. "Are they going to lock her up?"

As Mrs. Clark turned to go to her, an officer seized her by the wrist and twisted it.

"Come on, you," he said.

"You'll be all right, honey," Mrs. Clark said over her shoulder. "I'll be back in the morning. I've got that workshop to lead."

As she started quietly toward the door, Mac Sturges, a young white student from New York, intervened.

"Aren't you going to let this woman talk to a lawyer?" he asked.

"You're under arrest too," an officer said. "Come on."

Before they reached the door, there was another interruption.

Brent Barksdale, a slightly built young Quaker, had previously annoyed the Honorable Ab Sloan by following him around while he poked through the school library. Now he came forward again.

"How can you arrest Mrs. Clark when there's no liquor in the house?" he said.

"Don't you be following me," the officer said. "We know how to take care of little men like you."

And they did too, brave, brawny chaps that they were. They grabbed him by the seat of the pants and hustled him out to the car.

During the hubbub Guy Carawan had been sitting on the floor, strumming his guitar and watching it all. Now he broke into "We Shall Overcome," and rose to follow the procession to the door.

"You come on too," one of the men said.

They led all four of them to one car, put them inside, and

closed the windows. They were to sit there, on a hot summer night, for three hours while the raiders sought a solution to their dilemma.

They had a real one.

They had four prisoners, duly apprehended under the majesty of General Ab Sloan's orders. Among them was their prime target, Septima Clark. So far, so good. But there was one small problem.

They didn't have any evidence.

They hadn't found a drop of whiskey in the house.

"Hey," somebody said, "I know where they keep it. In the wellhouse. Let's look there."

They got the key and trooped over eagerly to conduct one of their justly famous searches. No booze.

It gradually dawned on them that Myles Horton's house was the only possibility. It didn't matter that Myles' house was off school property and could not conceivably fall under any search warrant authorizing investigation of school property. Whatever he had there was his own business. Myles was no teetotaler. He had never made a secret of the fact that, like practically every other adult male in Grundy County, he liked to take a drink when the time was right.

They got the key, after threatening to chop the door down, and moved in. Myles had liquor, in a cabinet which they broke into. Also, on the kitchen table, there was an opened bottle of rum and a half an inch of gin in a bottle, left over from God knows when.

On private property.

They also carried up from the basement a keg which sloshed vigorously. It turned out to be one that Myles had brought from Holland as a souvenir, which had been filled with water so that the staves wouldn't crack. They ransacked the house in their usual fashion, carrying off, for reasons not explained, one of Brent Barksdale's personal letters, rifling Guy Carawan's suitcase and boasting that they hadn't taken his money (as they had Septima Clark's), and photographing a copy of *Breezy* magazine which they found under Myles's young son's mattress.

They returned jubilant. They had their evidence.

Of course it had nothing to do with Highlander School, only with the personal habits of the Director in his free time in his own house, but that didn't matter. It had been obtained by illegal entry into a private home, but that didn't matter either. It was a physical object which could be shown to the judge, and that did matter a great deal. No matter how the deal is rigged, it's a little hard to conduct a murder trial without a corpse. And murder was exactly what the General had in mind. Murder of an institution.

Myles Horton, you will remember, was not a party to this suit, as Ab Sloan sagely remarked to the judge. But it was Myles's personal property, taken from his own house, which was used as the basis of accusing Septima Clark, a teetotaler all her life, of possessing "more than one quart of whiskey." Of such is justice, when this kind of justice needs to be done.

Back in the dining room the movie was finished and the group continued with songs. A quote from Reverend M. Petway, Pastor of the Ebenezer Zion Church, Montgomery, Alabama, sets the scene:

At the end of the movie we continued with our song services and, in singing, we sang "We Shall Not Be Moved," and at this point one of the officers seemed to become so interested and so disturbed about the singing that he tried to turn the light off and unconsciously turned the light back on before he decided what he was doing.

The students were not confused. They sang on until it was time for bed and, at that point, quietly retired.

Things were not so quiet down at the Justice of the Peace's office in Tracy City. The criminals had been brought in. All except Guy Carawan had ridden quietly.

"What are my rights?" he kept saying. "Don't I have any rights? What are my rights under the law?"

He got his answer from one of the troopers.

"If you don't shut up I'll bust you right in your damned mouth. And that'll be your rights."

From the JP's office they moved on to the courthouse, where they were fingerprinted, and then to the Altamont jail. Ab Sloan, doubtless wanting to see his chickens safely home, was also there.

"Did you get a good taste of that liquor, Septima Clark?" he asked.

"Why don't you test my blood and see?" she said. "Then you'll know for sure."

Curiously, her offer was not accepted, nor was a similar one by Brent Barksdale. Guy Carawan was too busy being heckled by the police to put his bid in. Mac Sturges' was not solicited.

Septima Clark was released, at 2:30 in the morning, on bond secured by Miss Vera McCampbell, a white school teacher in the community, and returned to lead the closing workshop on schedule. Miss McCampbell also arranged bail for the three men, but they were not released. All people apprehended on charges of drunkenness were required to spend eight hours in jail to sober up, they were told. The fact that two of them were teetotalers and none of them had had a drink was, of course, irrelevant, and they spent the night in the pleasant confines of the Altamont jail.

It was the first time that anyone had actually invaded the premises of the Highlander Folk School. There had been threats before. There was the time when C. H. Kilby, an employee of the Tennessee Consolidated Coal Company, an implacable foe of Highlander because of its assistance to workers in the county, organized the Grundy County Crusaders. Kilby, whom Myles had publicly described as a second-rate bookkeeper with delusions of grandeur, issued grandiose threats about coming up and cleaning out that nest of Communist rats. Somehow he never did. For one thing, Kilby was always more talk than do. For another, there was always a knot of the local boys, armed with shotguns and squirrel rifles, in the bushes outside the school on the nights when raids were announced. Myles didn't know this until much later, but the word got to the Crusaders without delay, and their enthusiasm rapidly diminished. The raids, perhaps because they lacked the dignity of the District Attorney General's support, never came off.

Since our account could use some humor at this point, it might be worthwhile to examine Mr. Kilby a little further. In 1963 he appeared before a hearing of the Joint Legislative Committee on Un-American Activities of the State of Louisiana. It was the usual kind of circus. By this time the Monteagle property had been confiscated and sold and Highlander was in full swing at the new Center in Knoxville, but Kilby came down to blast the Folk School anyway.

He now termed himself a minister of the Methodist Church and was introduced as the Rev. C. H. Kilby. He testified under oath that he had held a local Preacher's license for thirty years and was listed as a local Preacher in the Methodist Conference. *Concern*, a magazine published by the National Conference of Methodist Youth, had had this to say, in its October 23, 1959 issue, about Kilby: " The *Concern* staff has checked with the office of Bishop Roy H. Short of the Nashville area concerning Kilby's relation to the Meth-

odist Church. He is not listed in the annual conference report of the Tennessee Conference, and we were told that
there is no record of him as a Methodist minister in Bishop
Short's office."

Also under oath, Kilby offered some interesting facts.

One was the revelation that Myles Horton and James
Dombrowski had been members of Commonwealth College,
Mena, Arkansas. "In fact," he said, "it seems that's where
James Dombrowski came from and located in Grundy
County." James Dombrowski had come to Highlander, at
Myles Horton's request, straight from Union Theological
Seminary, a somewhat different institution, with no detours
at Commonwealth, and Myles, as we know, had never been
a member of Commonwealth College. Not that it would
have been a bad thing: Commonwealth, an avowedly Marx-
ist labor college, was a lively educational institution in the
thirties, as one of its more prominent alumni, Governor Or-
ville Faubus of Arkansas, once president of its student body,
could testify if the truth were in him. But for Myles to
squeeze this into the pace at which he moved would make
him even more of a miracle man than he has proved himself
to be.

This digression with the self-proclaimed Reverend Kilby
has a point beyond comic relief. His prime exhibit at the
Louisiana hearings was a series of fraudulent affidavits, the
gist of which was that James Dombrowski and Myles Horton
had been seen with Young Communist League membership
cards in their hands. Two of the affidavits were signed, full
name and all, by men who could neither read nor write; all
of them contained the same errors. For example, the name
of Ralph Tefferteller, a former Highlander staff member, was
consistently misspelled *Tuffy*teller. The accusation that he

had a Young Communist League membership card was the only thing that moved Myles Horton to indignation.

"If he's going to accuse me of communism," Myles said, "he might at least put me with the adults. The YCL is for kids."

Poor old Kilby didn't know any better. The Young Communist League was something he had actually heard about in the conspiracy he preached so steadfastly against. So he used it. Accuracy was not his line.

Having prepared the affidavits himself, Kilby set out to get them signed by one means or another. Sometimes it was by intimidation. Sometimes, it pains me to admit, out of my respect for the cloth, Demon Rum entered the picture. More than one signer waked up next morning, after a friendly gathering, to find his name, written by himself or the Reverend, at the bottom of a document he didn't even remember reading.

These documents had already been displayed at the Tennessee hearings, where they were accepted as gospel by Congressmen Senter and Rhinehart and Senator Dement, but to no avail. Kilby trotted them out again in Louisiana, to the awe of the local witch-hunters, and he offered an even more interesting piece of testimony which goes to the heart of the matter at hand.

On the last day of July, 1960, [he testified] G. F. Sloane [shades of Tuffyteller], our District Attorney, decided after we already had our State's investigation, and all of the witnesses from which I had originally received sworn affidavits, were summoned before the State investigating committee, and they found this school guilty of the same type of activity; but our Statutes of the State of Tennessee carried no penalties that could apply and get rid of this school. So, District Attorney Sloane figured out a raid might develop something down there by which we might get their Charter; that's what we were after, to run them out of business. So, we staged a raid with the help of our local Sheriff of Grundy County, and also the Tennessee State Highway Patrol, and they found that liquor was being sold there without a license, lewdness was being carried out promiscuously, and it was present when they made the raid; so therefore, they charged the school with all this kind of criminal activity, and we got through the Courts then, and got their Charter.

Under oath.

Representative James Pfister, Chairman of the Committee, was grateful for the testimony of so expert a witness. " Mr. Kilby," he said, at the conclusion of his testimony, " we certainly appreciate your taking the time to come here before the Committee. Thank you, very much."

This was the kind of mind Highlander was dealing with, and it was what they had to consider on the Saturday morning after the raid. The workshop was carried out in normal fashion: Septima Clark was not a woman to let little things like a raid or a trip to jail interfere with education. Afterwards, they discussed the problem. The workshop leaders, all of whom were leaders in their own communities, suggested that they prepare a tape of their reactions to the raid. Two comments will give a sense of the participants. The first is by Esau Jenkins, the moving spirit in the development of Citizenship Schools on St. John's Island, South Carolina:

Now I came here since Sunday, July 26, and I haven't even seen a bottle of beer in that drink box. The only thing in there from the time I have been here that I have gotten and have seen people have gotten out of there, that was grape, orange drink, and coke. I haven't seen anybody selling it, I haven't heard anybody ask anybody if you want to buy it. So that is false. And I will testify from here to heaven that that isn't true. And I had my eyes open. And if anybody was going to sell whiskey . . . I would have seen, but they didn't even have beer.

The second is from Dr. S. S. Seay of Montgomery, Alabama, who had been active in the Montgomery bus boycott and was the leader in insuring calm the night before:

Well, I arrived on the campus of Highlander on the evening of July the 26th. There were thirteen of us, together. I am Reverend S. S. Seay of Montgomery, Alabama, and there were twelve other persons with me. We spent the week here since the 26th. We had, as students here, a regular daily schedule that kept everybody busy on the campus, beginning from breakfast at seven o'clock in the morning. And from there we went to the assemblies where we spent most of the morning and most of the afternoon. During these assembly periods everyone that was attending the school was attending the assembly periods, listened to lectures and took notes of things that happened during these periods. I can say that there is not a single person that appeared in these assemblies that had any appearance of having had intoxicating liquors. There was no smell of it, there was no sign of it. All the twelve people who came under my supervision were directly under my supervision for the time they were here, and if any one of them had any intoxicating liquors, there wouldn't have been any way for them to escape my attention and my notice. I would have seen it and would have known. According to our schedule and the closely knit activities that were crammed way up, I don't think any persons could have been victims of drinking or subject of drinking or handled anything in the intoxicating line without others noticing it. And on the evening of July the 31st when the officers showed up we were having what customarily has been had during the institutes here, a banquet. We had several of the students to speak, several of the staff members to speak and what was served here did not appear to be, it was not, it didn't smell like, anything that had been in contact with any intoxicating liquors at all. We were quietly and peacefully looking at a film and a picture when the officers came, and the only panic that appeared was when some of the officers came unexpectedly on someone that was sitting on the campus. The other people went on their regular routine because there was nothing to feel guilty of, nobody had committed a crime, and during the whole process of the investigation there was no sign of anybody having been under the influence of intoxicating liquors.

That Was The Raid That Was. Only one further sidelight is necessary. Included in the raiding party were a photographer and a reporter from the Chattanooga *Free Press*, a long-time enemy of Highlander. It's too bad, from the point of view of their managing editor, that they couldn't have gone home with some redhot pictures and stories about lively interracial sin.

It should not be forgotten that the raid was conducted while Myles was out of the country. Myles had been around this part of the country all his life, and he had earned the respect he deserves, among other places on the picket lines we will consider later. These cheapskates had no notion of messing with him. But they had no fear whatever of roaring up in all those police cars — there were twenty troopers and deputies plus the newsmen — in the sultry Tennessee night to close in on an institution they had been instructed to finger now that the boss was gone.

There's an interesting paradox here which might as well go into the record because it illustrates the basic incompetence of these people, like Kilby's not even being able to get the name of his St. George — A. F. B. Sloan — or the year of the raid straight. They knew Myles was gone: nobody is away from a small mountain community for a week, much less six, without everybody's knowing it. That's why that bantam crusader for righteousness, our little old measly Attorney General, braved the raid in the first place, and it's why they came in shouting for Septima Clark. They wouldn't have risked it if Myles had been there.

Nevertheless, an item in the original bill read to Septima

the night of her arrest stated that on the thirty-first day of July, 1959, one Myles Horton was seen walking around the grounds of the Highlander Folk School with a bottle of liquor from which he was drinking. Anyone who knows Myles knows he couldn't possibly have done this, but that isn't the point. Truth was never of any consequence to the prosecution in this case. The irony is that, despite Myles's known absence, the flunky who prepared this document set this particular bit of fiction on a date when Myles had been out of the country for six weeks. Never underestimate the incompetent. They won.

Subsequent events followed a predictable pattern. Myles cut short his trip to Europe and returned to gird for the battle. In September a preliminary hearing was held — the one in which Ab Sloan called Highlander an *integrated whorehouse* — and the main building at the school was ordered padlocked because, the judge found, charges of selling beer without a license had been proven.

The facts about Highlander's distribution of beer are best summarized by Myles Horton's uncontradicted testimony — under oath:

I am personally responsible for having instituted a policy at the Highlander Folk School of having beer available for people who were there for conferences, the labor people who came, because I have always felt that we had no right to impose our students or ideas on other people in the community or neighborhood, and I wanted these people to stay there so I arranged to have it, much against the advice of a number of my colleagues and friends, I arranged to have beer available for people there at the school. When the groups would come and pay for it as part of their expenses, it was handled that way, and when they wouldn't, they had a rotating fund where people would contribute, put in some money in a box if they wanted to, and if they didn't want to, they didn't. And we used the money to refill the ice box when the Coca-Cola and beer ran out. This system was in operation up until, well, Mrs. Clark was against this kind of thing, and some of her other teachers are, and the last few years there had been very little of that.

Myles put it politely. The fact is that there was no place in Grundy County, although beer was legal there, where an integrated group could have so much as a coke together.

Highlander's activities, cramped by the loss of the main building but otherwise unimpeded, continued full steam ahead. In November the final hearings were held.

There wasn't any real doubt about how things would go. In the first hearing all the signals had been flashed. All but two of the state's witnesses had records of arrest or imprisonment. One of their stars, May Thomas, whose husband had worked at Highlander, had been ordered off school property for stealing. Once Myles, following a wheelbarrow path, even had to make a trip over to her house to recover some stolen dresses whose presence in her closet was a source of great astonishment to May. Shortly before the trial she had been arrested for stealing. One of her sons couldn't remember how often he had been arrested, and about the other May said, when asked what he was doing in Nashville: " He's in the state prison, but he ain't there for no communism."

May was the one who testified that she had seen a Negro man and a white woman having sexual intercourse on a couch in the glass-walled library designed by Carl Koch. The only trouble was that, at the time she mentioned, the library had not yet been built.

Judge Chattin regretted all this. " Sometimes," he said, " I wonder at the power of somebody to do something to a human being. Sometimes I shudder at what I have to do to enforce the law."

But he padlocked the school nevertheless, for a practice the Elk's Club and The American Legion had been carrying on for years and which Highlander had voluntarily discontinued a year before.

Against this backdrop the November hearings opened. If there was any doubt, it was resolved when the jury was chosen. Every juror admitted, under questioning by Cecil Branstetter, the chief lawyer for the defense, that he opposed integration, but Judge Chattin disposed of this with a simple question. " But you could put your opinions in your pocket and forget them, couldn't you? " he asked. Three long-time enemies of Highlander got on the jury, along with a cousin of a chief state witness at the previous hearing and a cousin of the sheriff who had conducted the raid. Justice would be done.

And was.

The context had changed a bit. All autumn Ab Sloan had been insisting that integration had nothing to do with the case. In an interview with *Concern* (the Methodist magazine mentioned above) he said, when asked if integration had anything to do with the state's case: " Not a thing in the world. It is immaterial who they teach and what they teach as it is within the law. It is up to the individual if he wants to socialize with colored people — I defend the law." A week before the trial, however, he amended his bill, contending that the Supreme Court decision banning segregation applied only to public schools, and that Highlander was guilty under an old Tennessee statute forbidding whites and Negroes to attend classes together.

So the integration question was finally out in the open, a fact that gave Highlander hope, since it seemed to provide a real basis for appeal to the Supreme Court. Branstetter opened the trial with a brilliant demurrer outlining the constitutional issues now that integration had been added to the bill. It was overruled. Both the Judge and the Attorney General had little law and cared less. They wanted to get on with the hatchet job.

The atmosphere of the trial is conveyed by an eyewitness's account:

Old Judge Rollings, formerly of that court, now past ninety, nearly blind, traipsed and shuffled around the courtroom daily, walking up between lawyer and witness, sitting at lawyers' tables, but most of the time plying the audience trying to sell copies of a paperbound book on his views and life, his loves and hates, etc. He looked like a big bloated superannuated frog on his last crawl. Dogs wandered in and out. Women with crying babes at breast attended persistently. No flag of any kind hung in the courtroom — not even Confederate.

In this august atmosphere Highlander Folk School went on trial for its life. There were nine charges, but the prosecution's efforts soon centered on one: that Myles Horton had founded and run the school for his own personal profit. Much of the argument centered on the fact that the school had deeded to Myles a plot of land and a house which he and his wife Zilphia had improved to the extent of $12,000 which Zilphia's father had left her. Zilphia had died, suddenly and unexpectedly, in 1956 and the Board, realizing that, since Myles had worked for nothing but subsistence for twenty years, his children would be penniless if he died too, deeded to him the house the Hortons had rebuilt with their own money.

The irony is that Myles had raised every cent involved in the school's operation and development and had never taken a nickel of it himself. He had, in fact, deeded the whole Monteagle property to the school, since Mrs. Johnson had

123

turned it over to him personally. But that's not the way Ab Sloan looked at it. Myles Horton had come to Grundy county for the sole purpose of building up a fortune, and someday he was going to slice the melon and eat it all by himself, piece by piece. Nobody accused him of slicing it yet: the facts were too clear. But someday, in the dark of the moon, he was surely going to do just that.

The jury agreed. Of the nine counts this was the only one finally submitted to them, and it took them less than an hour to decide that Myles Horton was guilty of running Highlander Folk School for private profit, in violation of its charter. In his final ruling the judge added the integration charge, since Highlander had never contested it, and the charge of selling beer without a license, since he had ruled on this at the previous trial.

Another round lost. But there were still two others to come, in the Tennessee Supreme Court and in the Supreme Court of the United States where, Highlander hoped, the question of enforced segregation in private schools would be given judicial review. Meanwhile Highlander had been legally ruled closed, on grounds which, even if true, made the Scopes trial look like a model of due process. Tennessee had again managed to cover itself with glory.

The flavor of the trial is best given by a brief excerpt dealing with Myles's trip abroad. His appointment as co-chairman of an international conference on adult education was an honor of which the state of Tennessee might have been justly proud. Here's how it went at the trial:

Myles — This trip was cut short because I had to come back here for a hearing — here. With great embarrassment I had to explain why this was happening in America with all this democracy, which I tried to do. I spent only about ten days at that conference.

Sloan — What explanation did you give them over there? What did you tell them?

Myles — Would you like to know? I'll tell you. I'd like to have that privilege.

Sloan — I'd like you to tell me what happened while you were over there — tell the jury what was so embarrassing to you. If you want to. . . .

Myles — I'd like to . . . I arrived there as co-chairman of an American-European Conference with participants from most of the European countries sending delegates from France, Sweden, part of Germany, Switzerland, Scandinavian countries, Spain and Italy. People from all those countries with newspaper clippings which they. . . .

Sloan — (objects)

Judge — You asked for it.

Myles — (continuing without a break) . . . showed me . . . an announcement for a hearing here, against a school that was integrated. They were from all these countries and they brought them (newspaper clippings) to the conference and asked why this could happen in a country that they had been led to believe was a democratic country. And as chairman of that conference, which I opened officially, I explained that we had a great country with great traditions and I was proud not only to be a citizen of the United States but also a citizen of Tennessee . . . that my ancestors were here long before most of us were and that I like Tennessee . . . and what was going on that they read in these papers did not represent the real tradition of Tennessee but that Highlander Folk School with its tradition of democracy and brotherhood was more in keeping with the tradition of Tennessee and the United States of America than the efforts of the State Legislature and other official bodies to harass a school that was integrated. And I asked them to consider the fact that we had a long history that was free of prejudice and the Highlander Folk School was in that tradition. I defended the United States and I defended our democratic system and I invited them to come to

125

the Highlander Folk School for the next European-American Conference two years hence and they accepted that invitation to be here and find out for themselves . . . to see what a good country we have.

Sloan — Are you through, Mr. Horton?

Myles — You asked for it. (laughter in the court room)

That's the way it was the whole way through to the preordained conclusion. Myles gave Sloan fits, but the General was always in command of the jury. Concerning the defense's distinguished witnesses — the Chattanooga *Times* observed that Highlander's witnesses were as impressive as the state's were unsavory — Sloan remarked to the jury: " And what did all those people who trooped in for Highlander really tell you? They just said, ' Look at me. Look how smart I am.' That's all they told you." The jury broke up in laughter.

The day after the trial some old-timers in the neighborhood came around to assure Myles of their confidence and support. One old fellow who had begun coming to Highlander dances twenty-six years before had this to say:

I know I'm dumb. I've been in more jails than hotels. But I've been through two world wars and Uncle Sam paid my travel. Those people at Tracy and Altamont are just plain ignorant. You've heard that ignorance is bliss. Well, they've got too much bliss. That's all they've got. Why those people are so ignorant they don't know whether Jesus Christ was crucified or run over by a truck.

Editorial reaction to this new stitch in the familiar pattern of persecution of Highlander was immediate. The Milwaukee *Journal,* writing in the ritual period between the jury's verdict and the judge's final decision, will serve as an example:

TENNESSEE PERSECUTES A SCHOOL

Most Americans look back upon Tennessee's famous Scopes trial in 1925 with either shame or a sense of incredulity. John T. Scopes was fined $100 for violating a state law against the teaching of evolution. The law and the finding of guilty brought ridicule and indignation down upon Tennessee.

Now local authorities, egged on by the state, seem about to present a simliar drama. The Highlander Folk School is being harassed by the state and local authorities and an effort is being made to revoke its charter.

The school, located at Monteagle, has been harried in many of its 27 years. Members of all races have gone to it for short periods to join adult education discussion groups, to study, to find guidance in their work. Highlander has attracted men and women from over the world — teachers, poets, musicians, philosophers. It has an international reputation and has been visited by outstanding leaders in many fields.

But Highlander has violated the code of the south — it is integrated! It has no bars of race, creed or color. It has been a source of help and solace for many Negroes as well as whites.

For this " crime " Tennessee authorities have made Highlander's life difficult. The legislature has investigated it. It has been charged with being Communist. It has been called a den of vice. But no charges could be proved — because they weren't true. Major state newspapers have defended the school.

Last July state troopers and sheriff's deputies raided the school and searched it. They arrested personnel, including Mrs. Septima Clark, director of education and one of the country's outstanding Negro women, on charges ranging from selling liquor and drunkenness to resisting officers. The charges were all trumped up.

This was shown when the state — in the county appropriately named Grundy — brought action to revoke the school's charter. The court would send to the jury only one charge — that Myles Horton, the school's president and founder, ran the institution for his own private gain. The jury sustained the charge. This in spite of the fact that for years Horton drew no salary and even now gets only $9,000 a year, a salary that several prominent educators testified was far below what the post should pay.

Now it is up to the court to decide whether Highlander's charter should be revoked on such flimsy grounds. But nobody is fooled by the case or the finding. There is only one thing at issue, and everyone knows it:

Highlander serves Negro and white students together on an integrated and equal basis. That is the "crime." It is for that that Highlander is being persecuted.

Letters of support poured in. But the case ground along its predestined course. The judge ruled as recorded above after denying a motion for a richly deserved mistrial. The Tennessee Supreme Court upheld the decision, taking pains to drop the integration charge.

The St. Louis *Post-Dispatch* saw it this way:

INJUSTICE IN TENNESSEE

The Tennessee Supreme Court's decision upholding a Circuit Court ruling that Highlander Folk School must give up its charter and shut down represents, in our opinion, a sacrifice of justice to local prejudices. This private center for adult education at Monteagle has been persecuted for the practice of racial integration. Yet the State Supreme Court ignored the Circuit Judge's reliance on a Tennessee segregation law which is clearly unconstitutional — a defect which should be ample to show the quality of the lower court's ruling and to invalidate it.

The school was accused of selling beer commercially, a trumped-up side issue similar to the spectacle St. Louis witnessed last December when a meeting of Americans for Democratic Action, at which there were some Negroes present, was raided by the University City police and the host, an Episcopal minister, was arrested for "selling liquor without a license."

Another charge was that Highlander's director, Myles Horton, violated the school's non-profit charter by accepting 76 acres of land and the home he lives in. In the narrowest technical sense this may have run counter to the terms of the charter, but hardly enough to warrant its revocation. It ignores Mr. Horton's testimony that the house was built with $12,000 from his wife's inheritance; it ignores his 28 years of selfless service to the institution he founded; and it ignores the whole character of the man, whose sense of acquisitiveness is so slight as to be almost nonexistent, as it had to be to enable him to spend so many years of his life between 20 and 50 without salary or expectation of tangible reward.

Though in a different place and in a different manner, Myles Horton has been performing the kind of service in the mountains of Tennessee that the late Dr. Thomas A. Dooley performed in Laos; he is off the same bolt of cloth. Highlander expects to appeal to the United States Supreme Court, and then, we hope, this unhappy and shameful business will be more satisfactorily settled.

Such pious hopes were to be frustrated, however. The United States Supreme Court, despite a statement by Archibald Cox, Solicitor General of the U.S. Department of Justice, that Highlander was " indeed making large contributions to both education and democracy and the closing of the school would seem to be a heavy blow to the public interest," did the only thing it could do. It declined to review the case. Once the Tennessee Supreme Court had eliminated the integration question — the only substantive issue in the case — there was no longer a constitutional issue for the Court to consider.

So Highlander was done, they thought. The charter was revoked and the property confiscated, including the house Myles and Zilphia had reconstructed with their own money. But of course it wasn't finished at all. The day after the Supreme Court refused review Myles went down and took out a charter for the Highlander Research and Education Center in Knoxville, same program, same students, same staff. They asked him only one question.

"What are you going to be doing there, Mr. Horton?" they said.

"Same thing we've always been doing," Myles said.

The charter was granted without delay.

One of the more delightful ironies in this whole shabby business is the action of the Internal Revenue Service. The prime charge which led to the revocation of Highlander Folk School's charter was that it was being operated for the personal profit of Myles Horton. As we have seen, this was the only charge submitted to the jury at Altamont. Nevertheless, despite this august decision by the judiciary of the great state of Tennessee, there has never been a single day in Highlander's history, from its incorporation in 1933 to the moment of present writing, when it was not covered by a ruling of the IRS describing it as a non-profit, tax-exempt, charitable and educational institution. On two occasions, once before the trial and once *after*, the ruling was suspended for an investigation. Both times Highlander was completely cleared, and the exemption was restored *retroactive* to the dates of incorporation.

It pleasures me to realize that the Internal Revenue Service, not a notably generous organization as far as tax monies are concerned, took the same view of Tennessee justice that I do.

Establishment of the new center did not, of course, spell an end to the attacks. Much as the Reverend Kilby might rejoice that this evil no longer existed in Grundy County, they didn't feel the same way in Knoxville. The Knoxville *Journal* took up the cudgels, with the usual non-results. The boys got on the growler, as I have mentioned, at the most inconvenient hours. Once at 3 A.M. Myles was awakened by an anonymous voice that informed him a bomb would be going off in ten minutes.

" I'm pretty sleepy," Myles said. " We've had a hard day. Call me, will you, and let me know what happens."

By the time I got to the center a routine had been instituted. We took the phone off the hook at bedtime and left it that way until morning. Sometimes we'd forget, though, and the calls would come through on schedule. These guys must all have asthma; at least, for non-talkers, they're the heaviest breathers I ever heard.

Petty attacks were the order of the day. When I called the Center from Knoxville, Alabama to say I'd be arriving next day, I was told that I could identify it because one of the white pillars was smeared with red paint. When I got there, both of them were smeared. The boys couldn't resist dropping the other shoe. Other favorite sports, conducted in a mood of playful fun, were puncturing tires with an ice pick when there was a large interracial gathering, and pouring sugar into gas tanks. You can't say the boys aren't inventive. They'd have taken the gate off the hinges and put it on the porch, only there wasn't any gate. They did enjoy roaring around the driveway late at night, and because of this more than one Knoxville garage has had the pleasure of replacing broken springs. There are some potholes on the further side of the house that have carefully *not* been repaired.

One other serious attack was to come. A whole book could be written on this one, but since it repeats the pattern of the Folk School raid and trials, we'll touch it only briefly. There is, however, one interesting variation.

On a property in Blount County, Tennessee, near Maryville and hard by the Great Smoky Mountains National Park, Highlander had set up a work camp. Buildings were being constructed to make this a permanent location for conferences. In the summer of 1963 the camp was under the di-

Thorsten Horton attaching lights at the camp which was raided in 1963.

rection of Mr. and Mrs. Robert Gustafson, another of the dedicated couples who gravitate toward a doing institution like Highlander. The evening of June 19th the whole party had been to a meeting at Oak Ridge and had arrived back at the camp after midnight. Around 2 A.M. the standard raid was conducted. The kids were getting ready for bed, laughing, funning, and talking over the evening's meeting.

This time the sheriff and his deputies entered private property with no search warrant at all — not even one like that used in the Highlander Folk School raid, which was so invalid the judge had to throw it out — and made the usual mass arrests. Liquor miraculously appeared, this time only a half pint; I guess expense accounts are meager in Blount County. The *pièce de résistance* this time was that a Negro boy, fully clothed, had been sitting on the bed of a white girl, also fully clothed, *talking*. Talking, for God's sake. Didn't these idiots know what they *ought* to be doing? The deputies did.

They were all marched down the mountain and thrown into jail. Not until next morning were any charges preferred. They included, to no one's surprise, disorderly conduct, possessing liquor, and, for the Gustafsons, contributing to the delinquency of minors. They were tried, in proceedings that must be read to be believed, and duly convicted. At the opening of the trial, for example, the judge steadfastly refused to admit evidence that the raiding party had been on private property — even though everyone knew it was private property — because, without a search warrant, the testimony would then have been inadmissible.

Highlander appealed. The twist is that it won the appeal. Not precisely through the courts. There had been offers of compromise along the way, on this order: if you'll agree the Negroes were guilty, we'll forget the convictions of the whites. A clean slate, wiped by the White Knight himself. Highlander refused, naturally, and when, after the expenditure of much time and money, the case was ready to be considered by a higher court, the General Sessions Court for Blount County made a remarkable discovery. It had all been a big mistake. The convictions were voided.

English translation: the judge didn't want to be reversed.

Following the convictions the vigilantes had taken over, against, of course, the dedicated resistance of the local authorities, and burned the camp to the ground. It was Highlander's second burning, but the first on property it was still occupying. When the main building at the Folk School was ignited it was after it had been confiscated and sold. Local folklore has it that a genuine whorehouse — not integrated — was being operated there, and that the burning, in the classic mountain tradition, had something to do with salvaging cash from insurance out of a losing operation. Like everyone else who has speculated about it, this deponent knoweth not.

Two items afford a proper ending to this tragic but wryly amusing history. One is the way the cows were sold.

Highlander had been experimenting with the development of a breed of cattle particularly suited to local conditions. It had accumulated a prize herd and employed a local resident to take care of it. This man came from a long line of farmers. In the manner of mountain people — parodied but immortalized in Snuffy Smith — his family had figured out the easiest way to do the job. He never called the cows in. He never seemed to pay them any mind, unless it was necessary, except at feeding time. Then he'd come out of the barn, lean against the door, scratch himself, and relax with a smoke. When the cows saw him there they'd know it was chow time and come gallumphing. Once they were settled at the feed troughs he'd go on about his business.

When the state took over, they hired a gang of local cowboys — Kilby's disciples, probably — to tend the cattle. At feed time they set out to round up the herd, yippie-yi-o and all. The cows were terrified. Nobody had ever talked to them like that, and they hadn't the slightest idea what was going on. Cows aren't very bright animals, but they do have one solution. They stampeded. They churned up pasture, knocked down fences, and in general put on a hell of a show. One cow literally ran herself to death, and it took hours to round up the others.

But it had a happy ending — for one insider in the proceedings. The cows were promptly labeled wild animals and he picked this prize herd up for a song.

I close with a letter from a local minister which is a model of Christian faith, hope, charity, and courage — Grundy County right-wing style.

I read what the *Tennessean* had said about the Highlander Folk School in three editorials since the matter has been under discussion. It seems to me the Nashville *Tennessean* leans somewhat toward the left, giving comfort to Communistic fronts. There is not a shadow of a doubt in my mind but that Highlander Folk School is and has been a Communistic front. It should be put out of business if for no other reason than for a nuisance.

John Church, now deceased, who worked there six or eight years, told me before his death that he could name eight young unmarried women who left there pregnant to become unwed mothers. He also told me that a preacher went there and asked to have prayer and he refused him. I think it can be proven that a young lady of Monteagle took some folks there and saw a crowd absolutely naked under the shade of trees. I understand Horton taught children there was no God. If he goes to church anywhere, I have never heard of it. When Horton comes to Monteagle he gets his mail, a stack of it, and darts out. That is a strange thing considering the time he has lived in this community. This man who worked there six or eight years said Horton was as mean as the devil.

This is a confidential letter. I am afraid of Myles Horton, and I think others are too, but I would like to see the school closed and Horton put out of business. Personally I think the school is a disgrace to the community. While there have been investigations of the school, the State Legislature has never done so, so I hope something good may come of this investigation. Confidentially.

He was afraid of Myles Horton.

He damned well should have been.

John Church set foot on Highlander's ground exactly once in his life — to fetch a young girl with whom he was living in sin right next door to his wife.

CHAPTER THREE

Community Organization

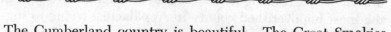

The Cumberland country is beautiful. The Great Smokies lie to the east, and the Cumberland plateau, the mountain of this story, falls a short way north of Chattanooga. It was, is, and, God willing, always will be populated by hill people. They are an indigenous folk, quiet and potentially violent, who go their own way, ask you no never mind, and expect the same courtesy in return.

When Myles Horton brought the Highlander idea into Appalachia in the 1930's, the area had already been raped. The people who give the country its character had made their living for generations in mines which had now played out and on farms which they had seen slowly go to rot. This had been a rich country, wild and fertile, the primeval country which was the gateway to American expansion to the farther west, but the speculators got hold of it and, in their usual fashion, did a systematic job of looting it. The mountain people never quite understood this. The good land was there and always would be; it was what you lived by. Then one day it was gone. The crops which had once flourished grew grudgingly, not enough to support one family on an acreage which once would have provided for a dozen. The mines were empty, stripped out, desolate; there was no work, and the people were hungry.

In 1935 Grundy County was among the first eleven counties in the United States in the proportion of its total population who were on relief.

This was the world Highlander stepped into. In this poverty-stricken country, Myles Horton, a country boy himself, began to preach a simple new message. Get together and talk things over for yourselves, he said. We may not have answers, but if we work at them together maybe we can figure them out. So Highlander began, a community center in the most impoverished county in Appalachia, trying to suggest answers for people who needed them. It was dry work. It's pretty hard to help a man whose farm is no longer producing or a miner who has been out of work for years to solve his problems. You don't buy a man bread, or sausage, or country ham, or even grits by giving him lectures: you've got to find a way to help him learn to deal with the problems he's faced with. This is what Myles Horton and Highlander Folk School set out to do.

At first people just came in for sociable evenings and talked about the things that were important to them. They came for fun too. Entertainment is sparse in the country, especially in the Puritan south, as anybody who has ever been a country boy there knows. Highlander was a place to talk, and have coffee, and sing, and dance the old dances that the local clergy had banded together to condemn as irreligious (among them the clap-hands dance that Governor Griffin made so much hay with), with the sets called by Ralph Tefferteller, whose name the Reverend Kilby was later not able to spell in his false affidavits.

But they did a lot of talking. It's hard for outsiders to

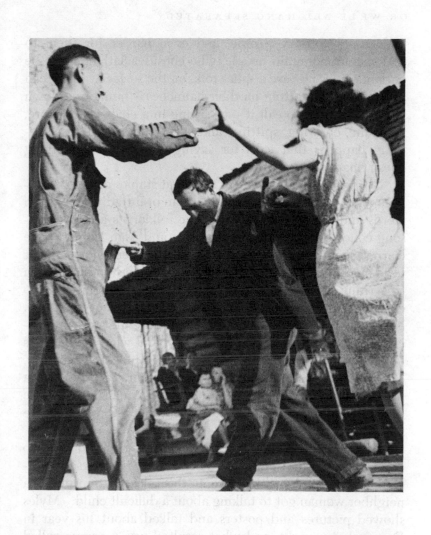

Folk dancing in the early days at Highlander Folk School.

understand country people, and even harder for them to understand mountain people, who consider flatlanders to be outlanders. They are a quiet folk, on the surface. They can sit for hours, squatting on their haunches — hunkering down is what we used to call it — or sitting in a chair in the store, whittling, chewing, spitting, and saying nothing until something happens that calls for saying. And that something doesn't happen very often.

Nevertheless talk is one of the great staples of their entertainment. These are a people with an oral tradition, both in words and music, which is why the folklorists and the folksong collectors, like John Jacob Niles and Alan Lomax, have learned so much from them. You have to keep things in your head in an oral tradition because nobody has codified them by writing them down. But the talk and the singing have to come at the proper time. You might even say the ritual time. No grown man would hunker down outside the store and begin to gabble. It wouldn't be seemly, and what is seemly is important to mountain people. It's the code they live by. They wouldn't start singing ballads either, or whip out a harmonica unless they were asked to. A man has to have dignity, and when dignity is all you've got left you treasure it all the more.

Highlander was a place where it was right to sing, to dance, and to talk. And they talked a lot. A course in psychology got underway because, in this relaxed atmosphere, a neighbor woman got to talking about a difficult child. Myles showed pictures and posters and talked about his year in Denmark one night, and what resulted was a course called cultural geography. When the miners' strike at Wilder, which we will examine in the next chapter, was at its height, a heated discussion of the issues brought on that class in economics. Highlander was coming alive as a place where people could discuss and begin to act on problems that were important to *them*.

Myles let things move the way they were heading. When courses developed where he needed help, he began to bring in consultants. One of the first was Dr. Charles Johnson, a sociologist and later president at Fisk, the fine Negro university in Nashville. He and Mrs. Johnson were the first Negroes to spend the night at Highlander, the first, in fact, in the modern history of the mountain, where the boast was that no Negro ever spent the night. They might work there during the day, but they went down the mountain at night. Dr. Johnson didn't. He stayed, and in that action the large history of Highlander is writ small.

In that first year Highlander, as a number of people have remarked, including Jane Addams, who should know, was more of a settlement house in the mountains than a folk school or an adult education center. The only trouble with this diagnosis is that it's wrong, as most pronouncements are. Myles Horton knew exactly what he was doing, down inside, that is, where it counts. He was letting a folk school develop in the only way it can develop, by serving needs that people arrive at by themselves.

Before proceeding to the bugwood strike, the first point at which community organization and labor education were manifested together, I'd like to pause for a document that fascinates me. It's a report by Oscar Guermonprez from the Volkhogeschool in Bergen, Netherlands. It was delivered at a Community Leadership Workshop at Highlander Folk School in 1955, and it speaks for itself. Mr. Guermonprez is telling, to an audience which included, besides people from the South, speakers from Sweden, Germany, Nigeria, and Panama, how the folk school idea got started in the Netherlands:

It's an interesting story, because that was in 1932, the same year you started here at Highlander. We started in the northern part of Holland. It is difficult, with the very dense population, to find a place which is more or less quiet and gives some feeling of being really completely far away from the largest — or not the largest — railroads. But we really found such a place. The man who found the place didn't intend to start a folk school, not at all, but it was a man who had been in his younger years in America here. He had been farming in the West, that was about 1903. He arrived in San Francisco just the day after this earthquake — that was his first impression. He lived there in the West and had this feeling of pioneering still. Later on he was in Australia, and was everywhere in the world.

He came back to Holland and sought for the place where there was the possibility still of pioneering. And he found the place. And later on he had his nephews, who were university students, and they all together spoke about these problems.

He first lived there quite alone but he was a man who had just found his place to be more or less alone. But he had all his experience of life and he had a wisdom in him, I think. So people liked to come to him. And there was no electricity, no gas, no water supply, nothing, you see, and they had no roads, no railroads — nothing. It was at least twenty miles from each railroad station. For our country, really it's quite a distance. I don't think there was one other place to find where this would be.

In winter evenings people came with a small lamp with oil in it, so they came in to find the way. They worked together in the old farmhouse and he'd tell them of America and Australia and all these things they were interested in. There was still in this region somewhat of the old neighborhood. For instance, when a person is going to die, then there is the neighbors who will take care of the corpse, will take care of the sick, will go with the cart to the cemetery and so on. It's not organized. It is an old form of real neighborhood still.

Then he started with some other things, first of discussion, and it became more or less such a citizens' club, you see. But never of the name — there was no name at all. But they were together and they got together since there were some special needs of this community. And they were trying to find solutions for them, so they talked about all sorts of things. They wanted something for the children and especially for the small. And they tried to find the girl who could take care of the children and started a kindergarten, which was a quite difficult task. And later on they came to do something for the children after their school time, and so it went on, and I guess it would be necessary for the women to have some lessons about cooking and gardening and so on, because there were very traditional ways of cooking. For instance, tomatoes and all such things were completely unknown and even many vegetables, and so to start it, they had to bring up the domestic science teacher. She started giving lessons in a very primitive way. It was my wife who started it. It was very difficult but it was good. There was no good, well-equipped kitchen to give lessons. That was a good thing, because they had to work in the same way as they had to work in their homes.

The folk schools started really from this community and so it grew. Some of his nephews, who were university students and who had studied sociology, said there is a need not only in this community but in the whole nation and they started this folk school work. And so that's the first. Now you will understand why I was so interested in coming here to Highlander.

Myles's comment was, "It's almost the story of Highlander." It was too, except that the Dutch had the sense to support the idea and the school had no Tennessee courts to contend with. Only German Stukas, and they survived those too, just as Highlander did the courts. Both schools remain thriving enterprises. As Myles remarked to the court, you can't kill an idea.

The importance of the parallel which Guermonprez's talk illuminates is that it goes to the core of what Highlander is all about. Technically, Highlander is a regional adult education school; its main focus is on the South. Yet the problems it deals with are of the utmost importance for our society as a whole; hence its national influence and support. It is useful to see this in an international context. These problems transcend not only regional but also national boundaries; they are the concern of all humanity. Viewed in this context, even a local incident like the bugwood strike takes on a new importance.

The bugwood strike was a failure, if success is measured only in economic terms. Nobody got a raise. The strike, which had wide community support, dragged on for months and then quietly faded away. The men didn't go back to work; they went on relief or got WPA jobs. The only positive economic gain was negative: no more wood was cut for the Tennessee Products Company and one further small piece of deforestation was halted. But the lessons learned by the community and the staff were of the utmost consequence, both for Grundy County and for Highlander Folk School.

The strike began spontaneously in the summer of 1933. The Tennessee Products Company, a Nashville firm, had contracted locally to purchase three hundred cords a day of cutover timber, known on the mountain as bugwood. Woodcutters were hired at 75¢ a cord, which worked out to about 75¢ for a ten-hour day. They furnished their own tools. One of the men was Dillard King. Another was Henry Thomas, the son of a lay preacher, who in his youth, before the forests had been cut out, had made good money as a logger.

"I got to figuring," Henry said, "that my pay amounted to 2½ cents a meal for the members of my family, so I went around to the other woodcutters and said to them, 'It takes a sharp axe, a strong back, and a weak mind to cut out bugwood at 75¢ a day. Let's strike!'"

They approached AFL officials for help in organizing but were turned down. They were not a very likely source for regular dues. So they went instead to Highlander.

Meetings at the school resulted in the formation of the Cumberland Mountain Workers' League. Within a week the majority of people in the community — in Summerfield, the village in which the school property was actually located; Monteagle was the nearest postoffice — had pledged " to be loyal to one another and to the purpose of the organization, which is: 1) to prevent the wholesale destruction of our forests; 2) to better the condition of the community by raising wages." This was a unique stand for a local labor organization which was later to be complimented by a TVA forestry service official, after the federal government had steadfastly ignored all pleas for help, on its method of preserving natural resources.

One woodcutter's comment at a Highlander meeting sets the tone of the affair.

" We really don't want to cut down the trees at all," he said, " but on the other hand there isn't any other work to do. It looks strange to me that the government would be paying CCC boys a dollar a day for planting trees at the other end of the county while we are cutting them down around here for seventy-five cents a day."

They did stop the cutting. Men, women, and children picketed the woods to prevent scabs from taking over. All of them memorized Section 7A of the new National Recovery Act, which guaranteed the right of labor to bargain through its own chosen representatives, and quoted it freely to anyone who questioned the strike. Recipients of this useful bit of information included a representative of the Tennessee Products Company who announced: " It's against the law to strike. You will all be in jail before the weekend."

They weren't, but they were never recognized by the company either, which turned elsewhere to buy timber for making wood alcohol.

The situation had its humorous aspects. When repeated pleas to various government agencies for help had failed, a delegation headed by Myles Horton and John Thompson, now a distinguished minister and an early staff member and longtime Highlander supporter, was sent to Washington. Their assignment was to lay the case before the Secretary of Labor. They made it to Washington all right, but they didn't get to talk to Miss Perkins.

" The Secretary of Labor," a staff member informed them, " is in conference with some important industrial leaders and cannot be expected to give her personal attention to every delegation of workers that comes to see her."

The boys from Grundy County were puzzled. They had the naive idea that labor meant workers, not industrialists. As they were to learn before long, however, the term could also include politicians.

Frustrated in their attempt to raise wages, the Committee turned to other ways of bettering conditions in a county where the average family income was less than $150 a year. An intensive series of classes on the history and organization of cooperatives was set up, following which there were experiments with cooperative gardening and canning. These too failed as the result of poor land and a dry summer.

Things looked bleak. By this time eighty percent of the approximately ten thousand people in the county were on relief. Out of 355 farm families, less than 7 percent were making a fair living. The remainder, plus the great majority of the 1900 non-farm families, were on the relief rolls. As Henry Thomas put it: " If it hadn't been for Roosevelt's relief we'd a'had to've cut bugwood. That's all there was to do. Cut that wood or just go hungry. They knowed we'd cut it for any price. Would if Roosevelt hadn't given us some relief."

Highlander had its problems too. Dr. Johnson, perturbed by Highlander's involvement in the Wilder strike and by the indignation of the small group of conservatives who ran the county, was having second thoughts about letting the school continue on her property. As the year's trial period was drawing to an end she went to Myles Horton and asked him what good he had done.

"Don't ask me," Myles answered. "Go about the community, go into the homes of the people and get your answer."

She must have gotten it: she renewed the agreement and subsequently deeded the property to Myles. Thereafter her loyalty to Highlander was unflagging. Seven years later — a good magic figure — she was issuing a press release, on the occasion of one of the numerous attacks, denying that Highlander taught Communist principles. "It's a labor school," she explained, "and attempts to help the labor people to better do their work and deal more intelligently with employers."

Things began to look up on other fronts too. Representatives of the Self-Help Cooperative Division of the Federal Emergency Relief Association, after a visit to Highlander, suggested that an application be made for a grant. With the help of an expert on cooperatives from TVA, a project was drawn up and a formal application was submitted. In March, 1935, the FERA made a grant of $7,000 to the Highlander Folk Cooperative. Enthusiasm ran high, but the people had their next lesson to learn. The conservatives swung into action.

Spearheading the attack was John E. Edgerton, president of the Southern States Industrial Council, an association which regarded the National Association of Manufacturers as dangerously radical. During his tenure as president of

147

the NAM, before his retreat back to a safer organization, he had rejected an invitation to speak at Highlander and had expressed his indignation in a letter to Tennessee manufacturers containing his classic description of Highlander as "the greatest insult ever known to Anglo-Saxon purity." Now he charged that the grant would be used by the school for "the teaching of un-American doctrines."

Like community organization and democracy.

You have to admit that Edgerton stayed in character. He had previously boasted that "I live in a section of the country in which the labor unions have made little headway and I do not hesitate for one moment to say to you that if it comes to choosing between a union man and a non-union man, all other things being equal, I will select the non-union man every time." Now he set out to make this doctrine stick in Grundy County.

Other champions of the status quo joined in the battle. On April 4, 1935, the Chattanooga *Times,* conveniently ignoring the fact that the Board of Directors of the Cooperative were local Summerfield residents, published this dispatch from Tracy City, the county seat, under the headline ALL WOULD-BE RECEIVERS OF $7000 U.S. FUNDS FOLK SCHOOL MEMBERS:

Resentful of aid for the Highlander Folk School, citizens in this community are moving against the institution. . . . It is not the cooperative movement here the citizens are protesting. Leading citizens insist they are anxious for needy and deserving families to receive all the benefits of the Federal Relief Program. . . .

They charged that none of the recognized leaders here have been taken in on the details of the cooperative movement. We have a relief organization in this county thoroughly capable of administrating the needs of the destitute. We had already planned relief projects and in the past years successfully carried them out, without the aid of a bunch of youngsters and irresponsibles. . . .

With the general belief that the Highlander Folk School will reap a lion's share of the net results uppermost in the minds of Grundy County's oldest and established leaders, a potential volcano is seething on the mountain — one which threatens an eruption without regard for the regular standards of law enforcement.

That one bears meditation. Needy and deserving families in the county knew the oldest and established leaders all right. They could smell them coming. And they were desperate enough not to be deterred by empty threats of lynch law.

But they reckoned without the politicians.

What was important to Washington, the folks in Summerfield now learned, as all of Grundy county was soon to learn through the WPA, was the state political organization. The Highlander Cooperative was too small to get out a significant amount of votes; the state machine could. The Tennessee Emergency Relief Association held up the grant, and the fight was on.

They even got Billy Sunday into the act, the noted evangelist who entertained me vastly when I was a kid in Georgia by racing around imaginary bases, preaching all the while, and sliding home with a run for Christ. He preached a special sermon about Highlander in a Chattanooga revival that spring. He was eloquent on the iniquities of reds and labor organizers and thundered in conclusion: "I protest the taking of the taxpayers' money to give it to a communist organization like this one out here on the mountain."

Somehow I doubt that he consulted Christ, even after that inside-the-park homer. As I remember, Jesus had a fondness for the poor. But old Billy, a frustrated minor league ballplayer, knew that Caesar was the side his rendering was buttered on.

I don't have to tell you who won. Ministers, teachers, organized labor, and other liberals lined up in support of the Highlander Cooperative, but in the summer of 1935, about three months after it had been authorized, the grant was withdrawn with no explanation whatever. Another defeat, but the community had learned a lesson. As Myles Horton summarized it years later:

The loss to the community was great but a valuable lesson had been learned. First, the people realized more clearly than ever that financial interests and trained-seal hirelings were the government in Tennessee; second, the support given by unions throughout the state and by friends of organized labor convinced the people that their only hope lay in becoming more closely identified with the labor movement.

This knowledge was to bear fruit.

Meanwhile Highlander continued to work on other fronts than the economic one. This series of setbacks could be expected to dampen enthusiasm, but the opposite happened. Morale among the working people in the community had never been higher. They had lost, sure, but they were used to that. But for the first time they had fought battles together, and their losses were victories compared to the submission which was all they had ever offered before. They'd lost the fight, but the important thing was that they'd *fought* it. So they came to Highlander on social evenings, all through this and after, and danced, and talked, and sang.

How they sang! Because something new had happened.

Singing has always been part of the Highlander tradition. Myles explains it by saying that any movement that means anything must have an emotional base and that singing is one sign that it does. Highlander tried from the beginning to act on this idea, but it wasn't easy. A singing people, as those in chains have always known, is a free people. Without spirituals, the condition of the Negro slaves in America would have been intolerable. It was bad enough, God knows, but music gave them the small escape valve they needed to survive. In singing together, something that old massa, Stephen Foster to the contrary, didn't know how to do, they found a weapon. It was one place that, poor, desperate, and oppressed as they were, they had something that was *theirs*.

The notion that spirituals represented a craven search for a religion out is as wrongheaded as most theories are. Religion was the form, but the essence was human solidarity, here and now.

But there's a funny thing about singing together. It's a different experience from formal music and it demands a special quality. Back on the old plantation the young missy was dutifully practicing on the spinet, but it was the Negroes in the slave cabins who were making the music. And don't deceive yourself that, as Southern folklore has always had it, it was because "darkies just like to sing." Slaves sang chained to the oars on Roman galleys too, under the lash. And Nubians were then in short supply.

Highlander found this out the hard way. Myles had professional musicians on the staff from the beginning, but it never quite worked. They knew all the motions, but the feel just wasn't there. What changed things was one of those happenstances that gives you hope.

Out in Arkansas there was a girl named Zilphia Johnson. Her father was a mine-owner. She had all the conventional training proper to a girl of her station. She went to the College of the Ozarks, majored in music, became an accomplished classical pianist, and won assorted musical contests in those parts. But a funny thing happened on the way to the conservatory.

She got interested in the labor movement.

This didn't sit too well with the old man, who hadn't expected to nourish sedition right in the bosom of his own family, and he booted her out of the house. Myles heard about it and invited her to Highlander in 1935 as a scholarship student. It would at least give the poor kid a few months' stopgap.

Only it didn't work out quite the way either of them expected. Myles fell in love with her and, with his customary celerity, married her. And, to their mutual surprise, he had found his music-maker.

It didn't come easy. Zilphia resisted at first. As a trained classical musician, she looked down on those country songs that fascinated Myles. But she sang them, and he sent her back to Arkansas to collect more, and a new chapter in Highlander's history had begun.

Because Zilphia had the one thing that had been lacking. Despite all the disadvantages of a conventional musical education, she had a way with people, and she could get them to *sing*. So she went on to become a legend in the labor movement and in the South, a woman, who, as John Thompson said at a Songs for Zilphia Memorial in Chicago after her death in 1956, " helped all the countless people she touched to make dark and dreary places throughout the South more human, more joyful, more songful, and gay."

He wasn't kidding about that *countless* either. Zilphia could get ten thousand people singing at once. And did.

So a new day had dawned at Highlander, one that was to have immense consequences for the freedom movement later on. But there were other immediate problems to be

Zilphia Horton playing and singing in the thirties.

faced in Grundy County. People were still hungry, and there was trouble with the WPA.

In the events that follow, the single purpose that pervades all Highlander's activities is manifest. From the very beginning Highlander had been involved in labor education. In November, 1932, Myles Horton first visited Wilder, where a violent mine strike was in progress. He spoke to the embattled strikers in Abe Nightingale's church and was arrested and run out of town for his pains. The charge was inciting to riot and " coming here and getting information and going back and teaching it." This was the strike that, as we have seen, led to Highlander's first economics course.

The organization of Grundy County's WPA workers, in which Highlander played a leading educational role, was certainly labor activity, a field in which the school was soon to become primarily involved. But it was also, and more significantly, an exercise in community organization. For the first time the poor people of the whole of Grundy County organized on a mass scale to deal with a common problem. And out of this organization there also came, as we shall see, successful political action, the first the people of Grundy County had ever experienced.

By 1936 it had become clear to the County's unemployed — which is to say the majority of the people — that a WPA job was about the only thing available to them. It wasn't much of a job. The $19.20 a month it paid could hardly be described as enough to support a family, but it was better than nothing. The reports from the venturesome who had sallied forth to the cities to find work were not encouraging. What they had found was not jobs but armies of the jobless, and they had come back home to take jobs with the WPA.

Even at $19.20 a month, it was far from clear sailing. Supervisors and foremen were political appointees, most of whom had little sympathy with the New Deal program. If you offended them, you were out of a job. They ran things their own way, ignoring government regulations. Although many projects required skilled labor, every WPA worker in Grundy County was listed as unskilled and paid the minimum wage. And working conditions were intolerable. "They treat us like a bunch of convicts," one old ex-miner said.

Then Highlander moved in. The school obtained copies of WPA Administrative Orders and distributed them among the workers. There had been a feeling that somehow it would be disloyal to organize on a government job, but it said right there in black and white that there were no rules against unions. Safety regulations were listed, all of which had been blatantly ignored in Grundy County. Workers were to be classified as skilled, intermediate, and unskilled, according to the nature of the job. A union, the men concluded, would not be against the government but would be a means of enforcing government regulations.

A local of the International Hod Carriers, Builders and Common Laborers Union was set up and grievance committees were established. Most of the immediate problems, except reclassification, were dealt with on the spot, and work proceeded more smoothly all around. Things were looking up.

But the honeymoon was brief. The union circulated a petition asking that, in order to permit a more flexible wage scale, the county be reclassified as industrial since, according to a TVA survey, only 7 percent of the population was engaged in agricultural work. It was signed by almost all the businessmen and officeholders in the county and passed on to Congressman Sam McReynolds, who promised prompt action. But it didn't sit well with authorities in Nashville, especially with Col. Harry S. Berry, State WPA Administrator. Complaints were ignored, unsettled grievances piled up, and appeals to Washington proved fruitless. Any favorable response from the government was ignored in Nashville.

The union's effectiveness dropped alarmingly. Non-union men were openly given preference on jobs. Foremen began to make fun of the union. The area engineer announced that he was getting damn tired of dealing with these union men. Membership dwindled. Something had to be done.

Having shown the men their rights, aided them in forming grievance committees, in drafting petitions, and in setting up protest committees which were ignored, Highlander now supported those who urged a strike. In early 1937, nine of the fifteen projects in the county were shut down by a strike. The demands were for union recognition with the assurance that grievances would be adjusted as they had been previously and for the replacement of the county administrator by a man "more honest and more human." The union also again urged immediate reclassification of the county.

Col. Berry's response was immediate. He replied not to the union but to the press. On March 13, 1937, the Chattanooga *Times* carried this story:

"A communistic organization has for months been feeding muscovite hops to relief clients in Grundy County," he said. "These clients are receiving the same wages as clients in other counties of the state of similar classification, and their monthly earnings are fixed in Washington.

"My advice to relief clients is summed up in the famous war time cartoon, picturing the British soldier, Old Bill, entitled, "If you know a better 'ole,' go to it."

A telegram from the strike committee to President Roosevelt in Warm Springs produced no results, but enough furor had been raised that a seeming victory was won. WPA officials promised that the union would be recognized and that grievances would be tended to. The men went back to work. Nothing had changed. The agreement was ignored, and the union's demand for the creation of skilled and semi-skilled jobs proved a two-edged weapon. Such classifications were made, but the better jobs invariably went to non-union men.

The mood of the men is illustrated by a paragraph from a letter to Harry Hopkins in Washington which the Highlander staff helped draft:

. . . Col. Harry S. Berry, State WPA Administrator, charges that we are protesting merely because we are being stirred up by some unnamed "communistic organization," and are being fed on "Muscovite hops," to use his own peculiar language. We ask you to demand that Col. Berry explain to us what he means by this, and to present his proofs. We deny these foolish charges. We do not appreciate such disrespect from a man who is supposed to be in office to serve us.

This didn't go down well in Nashville either, and a determined effort was made to break the union. At Laager, where there was a concentration of militant ex-miners, union men were ordered fired. When the county foreman, Charlie Adams, a union miner himself, refused to do so, he was fired along with the rest of them. The remaining men refused to act as scabs, and another strike was on. This one was won by a tactic which opened new horizons — appeal to the politicians. Congressman McReynolds was up for reelection, and the threat of an organized vote supplied the necessary prod. The union was recognized, and the strikers, who had not been deterred by the probability of a breadless winter, returned to work and proceeded to organize sawmill employees, truck drivers, and prop cutters. But they did not forget the lesson they had learned: politicians were on your side if you had the votes.

Highlander's role in all of this was typical of its approach and its philosophy. The men did the organizing, the protesting, and the striking. But Highlander had lit the fire, and it was constantly involved. It offered assistance, guidance, possible new approaches, any help it had the resources to provide. If direct participation were called for, it did that too. For example, when the WPA workers at Coalmont, all former members of the United Mine Workers, refused to join an AFL union, Highlander offered to set up a Workers Alliance local if it was agreeable to the miners. It was. Highlander also came up with the idea that eliminated possible competition between the two unions by suggesting that Dolph Vaughn, a key figure at Laager and a second generation labor leader, be made business agent for both organizations.

A thousand WPA workers, more than a tenth of the total population, man, woman, and child, of the county, were now union men. The people of Grundy County were dealing with their own problems in a democratic and united way. The next step, as they had learned, was politics.

On April 24th, 1938, Labor's Political Conference of Grundy County was formed, with Highlander's active assistance, to set up a political organization and run candidates in opposition to the county Democratic machine. Labor's candidates were all New Deal Democrats; the incumbents they opposed were conservatives who had the backing both of the County Committee and the Coal Company.

The campaign was bitter. The labor candidates were immediately labeled reds and a substantial campaign fund was raised to defeat this unexpected but certainly futile opposition. The union campaign fund was twenty dollars and scores of volunteers who tramped over the entire county soliciting votes.

It was a close race. When the votes were counted — and the unions saw to it that they *were* counted — labor had elected a sheriff, Roy Thomas, a member of the Miner's Union, by a margin of 218 votes; a school superintendent by a margin of three votes; and three road commissioners, one of whom, Charlie Adams, the former WPA county foreman who had been dismissed for refusing to fire union men, received the highest total vote and therefore became chairman of the Road Commission.

It was a grand victory. As Willson Whitman was to remark in *God's Valley*, apropos of this surprising occurrence in " a little lost county up in the Cumberlands ": " This is by no means a common occurrence; in fact there is probably no other county in the Valley's hundred where such a thing could happen."

Without Highlander it never would have happened. The Highlander idea, in action as always, had made the impossible possible.

Predictably, reprisals were not slow in coming. The sheriff's salary was reduced from $800 to $400 and his mileage allowance was cut off. The Tennessee Power Company shut off the lights in the county building, and the sheriff was warned that he would be starved out unless he resigned. The union came to the rescue by voting a small assessment to enable Thomas to continue in office.

The road commissioners were in trouble too. E. E. Hampton, president of the Tennessee Consolidated Coal and Iron Company, who had for years run Grundy County from Nashville, and Col. Berry, who as WPA Administrator now controlled the largest number of jobs in the county, had no intention of letting their authority be undermined by a petty local rebellion. Charlie Adams, an ancient enemy of these " bosses," was now the officially elected representative of the county in dealings with the WPA. In this capacity he arranged, in a meeting with Congressman McReynolds and the District WPA Supervisor, to present a list from which new foremen and timekeepers could be chosen to replace the present political appointees. McReynolds confirmed the agreement in writing in a letter to the WPA.

Nashville ignored it, and a systematic campaign of harassment began. Although the road commissioners were the custodians of county machinery, men, including a road grader who had previously been fired for drunkenness, were put to work on it without their knowledge. It was the commissioners' responsibility to designate the roads to be worked, but men were regularly shifted from one road to another without their knowing anything about it. A lock on the county storage room was changed so that the commissioners couldn't enter. Complaints to Nashville were ignored. Finally the commissioners notified Nashville that if the agreement could not be lived up to the contract between the County and the WPA would be cancelled in thirty days.

Berry ignored the letter but responded, as usual, to the press. On January 17, 1939, the Nashville *Tennessean* carried the following story:

A conflict between the Grundy County Highway Commissioners and the WPA threatened today to close the WPA Farm to Market Project which employs 700 men in Grundy County and provides the sole income of an estimated 2500 people.

Harry S. Berry, State WPA Administrator, announced today at Nashville that he had received notice from the county highway commissioners terminating effective Saturday, the contract under which the Farm to Market program operates.

Berry stated this afternoon that he would not wait until Saturday but would withdraw all WPA support " immediately " but tonight gave word that he would not close the project down if the three highway commissioners would resign before Saturday.

COMMUNISM CHARGE

Charges of "Communism" were made by Berry as he charged in a statement that the highway commission has attempted to build roads by the hammer and sickle rather than with the pick and shovel.

Harry Berry, moneybags in hand, had no intention of dealing with Charlie Adams, and if the people of Grundy County suffered for it they could find a better 'ole.

The commissioners refused, on the grounds that the Colonel had no right to demand the resignation of duly elected local officials. Conferences proved fruitless. Berry was adamant in demanding the resignations as the price for reopening the project. The men stood behind the commissioners. Much as they needed the work, they had worked hard to elect their own representatives, and they weren't about to give up their hard-earned victory.

Berry had also put himself on the spot, however. As State Administrator he had to provide some kind of project in Grundy County or be in trouble with Washington. So he opened a smaller project, employing about three hundred men, on the state roads in the county, thus bypassing the county commissioners. Almost all the men hired were non-union. In well-organized communities like Summerfield, the WPA even trucked in men from twenty miles away to replace local workers.

Even the unorganized, who knew they had benefited from the union's gains, couldn't take this one. They joined union members in demanding a strike and promised that every project in the county would be shut down. But Highlander and Dolph Vaughn had a better idea.

At this point a strike would only play into Berry's hands. He could then claim that the people of Grundy County were refusing to work and close down the projects on what would appear to be reasonable grounds. In a stormy meeting Vaughn finally persuaded the men not to strike. The few union men who had been hired would go to work as usual and those who had not would go to the relief office and demand work cards. It was well after midnight when the meeting broke up and the men set out on what was for many a six to eight mile walk home.

Next morning a selected group of men entered the relief office in Tracy City, which was housed in what had once been a church, and asked for work. They were told that there would be none until more projects were started. They left quietly, but in a few minutes they were back. Two men carried an oil stove. Others followed with bags of potatoes and onions. After them trailed their wives, carrying pots and pans. Calmly and methodically, they set up housekeeping in the middle of the relief office, where the air was soon fragrant with the aroma of a meatless but savory stew.

The County Administrator was flabbergasted. He scurried to the sheriff, union man Roy Thomas, and was assured that all violators of the law would be arrested. To ensure the peace, Thomas deputized Dillard King, president of the Workers Alliance, and two other union officials. Meanwhile the stew cooked sweetly on, and was consumed with relish by a crowd that now numbered over a hundred. As the Chattanooga *Times* reported from Tracy City on February 10, 1939:

J. V. Walker, Grundy County WPA Administrator, said tonight that approximately 150 men and women, former employees on relief projects, had moved into the building used for relief headquarters here with the announced intention of staying until they were given jobs.

Next day there was another story:

A parade of an estimated 500 WPA workers demanding food and work cards was held here this afternoon under the leadership of Dolph Vaughn, business agent of the Grundy County Workers Alliance. The parade followed a short mass meeting in front of the relief office where some 300 men were fed by the union at noon. . . .

With an oil stove in the relief office, 150 men spent the night there and the crowd grew throughout the day. Vaughn said the men intended to remain in Tracy City until action is taken to correct the WPA situation.

They had a ball. The office became a combination club room, relief kitchen, and dormitory. Local merchants, who needed those dollars and who didn't cotton to highhanded interference from Nashville anyway, donated food, money, a coal stove, and a tent. Highlander campaigned throughout the county and appealed for aid to unions and friends all over the country. This sit-in was solidly in business.

Outside on the lawn, cooks bustled around the stove, serving meals twenty-four hours a day. Inside they played cards, sang union songs, told tall stories and gossiped and watched skits put on by Highlander staff members. They even had their own mimeographed newspaper, *We, the People*, a couple of excerpts from which will give the tone of the assembly. One is from an article, "We Shall Not Be Moved":

The securing of work cards will be the only thing that can remove the jobless from the relief office, judging from the spirit of the meeting held here Friday night. Organized labor has taken over the relief office and intends to stay until they get their jobs back. After a tasty dinner of good old Irish stew and coffee, the group held their first meeting and committees were set up.

The second is a " News Flash ":

WPA office at Tracy City running full time, day and night — 24 hour service — meals served — everyone having a good time — three card games going at 90 miles per hour — cooks very busy — about 100 present — 3 union deputy sheriffs and some WPA officials.

The workers were set to last out the winter, but they got only a week. Nels Anderson, Director of Labor Relations of the WPA, came down from Washington, and in a day-long conference with the local WPA officials and the two Grundy County unions, it was agreed that jobs would be provided and that the men would go back to work. It was a victory, but it was one that paved the way to eventual defeat. The men were assigned to state projects. Col. Berry still exercised the privilege of not dealing with the road commissioners.

By this time the community as a whole had realized that the problem was theirs as well as the union's, and a mass meeting was held. A steering committee consisting of the local postmaster, Clarence Kilgore, the Coal Company Superintendent, Everett Roberts, and Myles Horton was appointed to deal with various relief agencies. A broadly based Citizens Committee was also formed. A meeting with WPA officials, in which the commissioners participated, resulted in a mutually acceptable contract which would permit the Farm to Market projects to be resumed. Col. Berry refused to sign it.

Over the protests of the union, another mass meeting was held, with the obvious purpose of reconstituting the Citizens Committee in a form more acceptable to the Colonel, that is to say, without representatives of Highlander or labor. A Mr. Swan, a Coal Company official, was elected temporary chairman. Swan was eloquent in his praise of Colonel Berry, who had told him, he assured the audience, that he would take care of every man he could even though he could not deal with the road commissioners. "I played with Harry Berry when he was a boy," he said, "and despite the fact that Berry is a blueblood, he never considered himself above the poor boys."

Only above road commissioners who dared to disagree with him and "reds" like the folks at Highlander.

Two committees were finally formed, one in Berry's image and one in the unions', the idea being that the two committees would then elect representatives to a Coordinating Committee. This awkward non-solution was prompted by the county welfare director's saying that it was time to face what he called the real issue: the citizens, he said, were convinced that nothing constructive could be done as long as representatives from the School or influenced by the School were allowed to serve on the committee.

That took in a large part of Grundy County.

The conservative committee never got off the ground. The union committee did manage to start two community gardens which helped support 28 unemployed families. But the battle by Grundy County Citizens to control their own destinies had been lost — not in the county, where victories had been spectacular, but in Nashville and Washington. Congress was busily hacking away at WPA appropriations and Berry and his subordinates took advantage of the cutbacks to eliminate union men from the projects. Membership in the WPA unions declined drastically: unemployed men can't afford to pay dues.

There was a lesson here, one Myles Horton was to ponder for years, during all the time the school was primarily engaged in labor education and in work with the freedom movement. The answer, when it came, was as simple as all right answers are. Occam's Razor, as modern scientists have discovered, still applies: of all possible solutions, choose the simplest. The simple answer here was that, no matter how well they are organized, no matter how active an interest the citizens take in their own affairs, a small local community or a county is not a large enough base. Colonel Berry could continue his authoritarian practices, despite all his defeats on the local level, because in the political and economic power structure Grundy County wasn't big enough to matter.

In that answer, as we shall see in the epilogue, lies the current step in Highlander's single-minded but continuously evolving history.

CHAPTER FOUR

Labor Education

When Doctor Lillian Johnson told the press that Highlander was not a Communist institution, just a labor school, she was almost right.

Communist it never was: she was right about that. But it wasn't just a labor school: about that she was wrong. It was a people's school, a Folk School. Most people are working people, despite the wishfulfillment of American advertising. The average housewife doesn't spend her time explaining to her neighbor that the latest detergent washes *cleaner* or that this new wax is scuff proof. She worries about what she's going to serve on Sunday, and if she's poor — and there are plenty of poor in the Affluent Society — she worries about how the hell she's going to scrape up the money.

Since Highlander has always been dealing with people, initially the working people of Summerfield and Grundy County, it quickly got into labor education. If Highlander's activities at the Wilder Strike in 1932 prompted its first economics course, you can also say that the need for its first economics course prompted its work there. The Highlander idea has always been that you deal with people in the situations they are *in* and do what you can to help.

So Myles Horton went over to Wilder. He made an eloquent talk in Abe Nightingale's church and was run out of town, as previously reported. But it didn't end there. What has never penetrated the thick skulls of Highlander's opponents is that an idea doesn't die. Highlander came back, by the people's request, for months to come.

Maybe I should pause here for a comment. When people, even unto General Ab Sloan, mistakenly called Highlander Communist, it doesn't mean they had the wrong idea. They just had the wrong label. Highlander has always been the most seditious institution I know. That's why I love it. And that's why the people of Appalachia loved it. It spoke for the democracy they had come there centuries before to believe in. And it still does.

At Wilder, Highlander moved into an explosive situation. It was a lockout, technically called a strike. And it culminated in murder.

To understand this, you have to have some sense of the mood of the South in the thirties. It was as violent as it is now, but the targets were labor leaders, not civil rights leaders. These were then the offenders against Southern white purity.

The target in Wilder was Barney Graham, native Scotch-Irish (my own breed), poor white. He was a semiliterate, brilliant organizer with an enormous empathy with people, and he had committed the absolute sin of leading a strike against the Fentress Coal and Coke Company. They set out to get him, in their usual fashion, and they dynamited a little bridge and accused Barney of doing it. Everybody knew that if anybody really wanted to do something they'd dynamite a useful bridge, but the charge was enough to have the Governor of Tennessee send in the National Guard, including cavalry, at a cost far exceeding what the Company had ever paid the state in taxes. There were protests, because sending troops was clearly unconstitutional, but the militia weren't withdrawn until a new governor was elected. Meanwhile Barney had been murdered.

It's important to understand this context, but it's hard to communicate to somebody who hasn't been there. I remember, for example, Gene Talmadge, the red-suspendered Georgia Governor, whose boast was "Ain't nobody done nothing for the people of Georgia except *Jesus* Christ, *Sears* and Roebuck, and *Eugene* Talmadge," putting the National Guard up behind sandbags on top of a cotton mill right across the street from us. The strikers were puzzled. Old Gene was the poor man's friend, and they didn't understand he'd been playing footsy with the mill owners all along. But they figured it out, which is how Georgia got organized. I remember too grabbing a cop's billy outside Churchill Downs in Louisville, Kentucky, and whacking him back with what he was going to brain me with. I had only been exercising the immemorial privilege of all kids who knew a stable owner or plater to sneak through the fence and watch the derby from a privileged perch on top a barn. War Admiral, that beautiful little black horse, won that day, and nobody came close to him. After I got through the fence, the cop went after somebody else. I hope he didn't get close to them either.

The point is that our people have always hated the fuzz. The kids the state sent into Wilder were like the ones now misrepresenting us in Vietnam and too much of the rest of the world, accidentally shooting kids who are shining their shoes or raking down women and children. Trigger-happy children who got their first feel of power when they had a gun in their hands. The strikers at Wilder didn't cotton to it, and Barney Graham didn't take to it either.

It was public knowledge that his murder was scheduled. Myles Horton and Alva Taylor, a Professor of Christian Ethics at Vanderbilt, presented the facts to the Governor and even named his intended murderers, who turned out to be precisely the guys who did the job. The Governor, who had no hesitation in sending in troops at the request of the coal company, couldn't see that he was constitutionally obligated to protect Graham on the basis of such vague charges. When they killed him, eight days later, on the main street of town, they fired ten shots into him, four of them into his back after he had fallen dead. He lay in the street three hours before union men were permitted to take his body to a doctor. His assassins were Shorty Green and Doc Thompson, both imported employees of the coal company. They claimed self defense, after also beating Graham in the head until his brains ran out, and were duly acquitted by a local jury after an hour's deliberation. They planted a gun on him, after he was dead, but they didn't have the sense to take off the safety catch. No shot had been fired from it, as even a deputy sheriff, Dick Stults by name, testified.

Shorty Green's attorney was appropriately nicknamed " Bully " Garrett.

What the miners were protesting was very simple. Under the union contract they had been paid $2.00 a day. Now they were being asked to take a 20 percent cut. Unchanged would be the following monthly deductions:

$1.50, per room for a company shack
$1.25, for bathhouse; company houses had no running water or bathing facilities, and all water used at home had to be brought in buckets from five village pumps
$1.50, hospital

$1.53, doctor
$1.00, funeral
$5.00, powder for blasting
$ .38, blacksmith
$1.00, tools
$1.25, lights, for the minimum rate of ten kilowatts.
       10¢ per kilowatt after that
$1.90, coal, required to be paid twelve months a year
$1.35, hauling coal

In addition, they were paid in company script, which made it necessary to trade at the company store, where prices were like this: 95¢ for a bucket of lard which sold elsewhere for 65¢, 50¢ for a pound of cheese that sold for 25¢ elsewhere. A new miner was paid nothing for a month and five days, by which time he was in so deep at the company store he could never get out of debt.

Start taking all that out of $1.60 a day, the proposed new wage, and see what you're left with.

There was nothing, the company told the press, to arbitrate. Take it or leave it, boys. Or find a better 'ole. Of course they could use the National Guard at a cost to the state of $32,000. They couldn't depend on deputies any more, except for murder, despite Sheriff Peavchouse's convenient habit of signing blank deputation papers and giving them to the Company to fill in however they wanted. Two of which went to Shorty Green and Doc Thompson, hired gunmen.

Even the Red Cross got into the act. The local secretary was Mrs. L. L. Shivers, wife of the mine superintendent. She dutifully supplied flour and cloth to the scabs but not to the strikers. This was righteously denied by Mrs. Shivers, but Myles Horton, in his systematic way, had gone to the trouble of getting a few affidavits. One of them will make the point:

State of Tennessee
County of Overton

I, Luther Hodge, having been duly sworn, state that in the spring of 1933 I saw a notice on the bulletin board of the Company Store in Wilder saying the Red Cross cloth would be given out only to employees of the Fentress Coal and Coke Company who wanted it; this notice was signed by Mrs. L. L. Shivers. During that same spring I saw, on many occasions, workers in the Fentress Coal and Coke Company's mines carrying home Red Cross flour from the Company Store. I never saw nor heard of a striker getting Red Cross flour or cloth from the Company store although many of them needed help badly.

Luther Hodge

Sworn and subscribed to before me this the twenty-first day of May 1934.

J. R. Copeland
Notary Public, Twinton, Tenn.
My commission expires in October, 1936

There is no record of any affidavit which Myles either made or procured ever being successfully challenged.

The only temporary setback the Company suffered was when Squire Thornton Wheaton ruled that seventeen strikers could not be evicted from company houses because the warrants were served by officers in the pay of the Company and that by law no officer could serve warrants in cases in which he had an interest. Speaking for the Company, counsel W. A. Garrett replied in the classic manner: "I have never heard," he said, "of a case being dismissed on such frivolous, nonsensical, and unintelligible evidence."

Company counsel aren't much interested in law. Only results.

The fire went out of the strike after Barney Graham's murder, and the men reluctantly went back to work on the Company's terms. But it wasn't all loss. Highlander had helped, in its accustomed way, to give people a sense of having done something together. Maybe the best sense of the situation is in Dr. John B. Thompson's account, in *American Folksongs of Protest*, (University of Pennsylvania Press, incidentally, so we can keep this protest as respectable as possible, though I don't feel much like being respectable when I have to write about good men being murdered and their brains beaten out) of how he recorded the text of " The Wilder Blues ":

In January or February of 1933 I went down to the Highlander Folk School to help Myles Horton to get his school started. The whole school had a budget of $1400 for the first year; we nearly starved, literally. But that's another story.

One of the first services we performed was at the lock-out of the miners in a little valley town, Wilder, Tennessee. There was nothing in Wilder but the coal mines, the miserable little shacks the company rented to the miners, the company store, and one or two sad, unpainted churches. The miners worked hard and dangerously, but sank deeper and deeper into debt. They didn't have enough to keep their children alive, so finally they went out on strike. They were affiliated with no outside organization; they just had a little union of their own.

When they struck, the company turned off the electricity and took the doors off the houses. It was midwinter and terribly cold. But still the company could not break the morale of the union, which was led by a mountaineer named Barney Graham. To " protect property " the governor sent in the National Guard. These young soldiers were fresh and cocky; they had never had authority before; they got drunk, they swaggered, they incited the strikers. Then the company brought in strikebreakers —

scabs. We saw the advertisements the company ran in mountain newspapers and circulated in handbills. They offered the scabs much better wages than they had paid the strikers, board and room, guard, and "a woman at night." So they got plenty of scabs.

Myles discovered this situation and wrote letters which were published in the state's leading newspapers calling attention to the plight of the strikers. A little group of Socialists in Nashville gathered food and clothing and a little money, which Myles and I hauled over the mountain roads into Wilder every Saturday. I will never forget the long line of gaunt, haggard, brave people who lined up to receive the scant rations we handed out to last them a week. Each family got a pound of dried beans, a half-pound of coffee, two tins of canned milk (if they had a baby), half a pound of sugar. These rations saved many lives, but meanwhile many babies had died of starvation.

The company had let it be known that if Myles ever came back he would not get out alive. But the next Saturday I drove him back into town and we distributed the stuff again. We were unarmed. When we went into the company store about a dozen scabs put their hands on guns, but the strikers followed us around and about two dozen of them fingered their pistols. So we walked around innocently and safely, like Ferdinand.

One very cold Saturday, after giving out all our groceries, we went into a stuffy, dirty little frame hotel where a poor meal was put on a long table, and for fifty cents you could sit down at the greasy table and help yourself along with anyone else who had fifty cents. While I ate I heard music and commotion in a front room, a bedroom. I edged my way in. A man, about fifty or sixty years old, wearing an old black hat, and with a two-weeks beard, sat on the bed strumming his guitar. As he played he sang stanza after stanza of a song he had composed about the Wilder strike. (The mines were at Davidson and Wilder.) Whenever he ended a particularly good stanza, the men — twenty or more — would cheer and say, "Uh-huh!" or "Amen!" He made some new stanzas in my presence, but when he saw me and my city clothes, he stopped. I told a union official I would very much like to write the song down. They asked the bard, Ed Davis, but he was timid and refused. I begged a bit, but it did no good. So I went outside and got a couple of dirty little kids who were running around the house, and told them to go in and ask Uncle Ed to sing it again. Ten minutes or so later they did, and it worked. I sat outside the door, most of the men realizing what was happening. The kids begged him; he sang it again and I got the chorus and some of the stanzas. Then I had them go in and ask him again, and that's the way we worked it; he just kept singing it for those kids and the fellow strikers who sat around cheering him and joining in the chorus. Finally, I got it all down and had the tune well enough in mind to go back to the dining table and write it down. Then the men told him I had written it down, and to my surprise, he was very much pleased. He had just been too selfconscious to sing it for me. Two weeks later we had Norman Thomas come down to speak at a mass meeting. We had Ed sing the song again and the audience cheered and ate it up. It was their song; it was their life.

Ed Davis, who wrote this song, could neither read nor write, but he sure could play that guitar."

Highlander's attitude is summarized in this story from the Chattanooga *Times*, November 29, 1932. I'm especially fond of the headline:

MYSTERY TEACHER SLAPS GUARDSMEN
DESCRIBES DRINKING OF SOLDIERS AT WILDER

Mystery surrounds the location of the "Highlander Folk School" and the exact identity of its director, Myles Horton, who was arrested by national guardsmen after visiting the mine strike area near Wilder last week and later released.

. . . . .

In his letter, Horton alleges that he was arrested because he "had been seen in the company of union officials." He continues:

"Some time ago the people of the south protested the visits of investigation committees from the east at Harlan, Ky. If my experience is typical, not even local people are allowed the privilege of knowing the truth about labor troubles. I was arrested and the notes I had taken of the situation were read. I was charged by Capt. Crawford with 'coming here and getting information and going back and teaching it.'

"No trouble occurred while I was at Wilder," the writer continues, "but three people are willing to sign an affidavit that two drinking child-soldiers boasted that they were there to 'get Barney Graham,' president of the union. Drunkenness among the higher officers is common. While I was under arrest, an officer took a bottle out of his pocket and handed it to another officer before proceeding to question me.

"The miners are living in constant fear that some drunken soldier will kill their wives and children with the high-powered rifles they are carrying. The only thing so many soldiers can do is to cause trouble with the strikers. This would give the company a chance to arrest the union leaders and break the strike."

They found out soon enough where that little old school was, and Myles Horton ceased to be a mystery. Just an enigma. But Highlander had also found out something. Community organization in Appalachia inevitably involved labor education; any folk school had to become a labor school. The problems in the region were basically economic. Until people could band together to solve them they didn't have much chance to think about anything else.

This realization was to set the school's course for the next twenty years.

Highlander was so deeply involved in labor education in the South that a full account of its activities would take another book. Without Highlander, the CIO's rooting in the South would have taken a much different and slower course. So let's just take a few examples. We'll begin with the Lumberton, North Carolina, strike.

The Lumberton strike was a grim one. At the time Myles was on leave from the school, working full time as an organizer for the CIO Textile Workers Organizing Committee. It was the first big breakthrough for the CIO in the South, and despite the unimportance of Lumberton, a lost little town near the South Carolina border, it was an important strike, the first in which an NLRB decision was made. Myles had just come from organizing the mills in McCall, South Carolina, where the problem had been much easier.

It was also one of the most hilarious strikes in American labor history, entirely because of Myles's inventiveness.

One of the first things he did was to institute a new type of picket line. When the fuzz roared in, as they predictably did, he called the regular pickets off the line and substituted a few pretty girls and local banjo and guitar players. There even might have been a stray harmonica player.

The cops loved it. Pretty girls are pretty and music is always good. When the cops left town, Myles threw back the regular picket lines.

The banjo and girl routine didn't last long. The mill owners got the idea and insisted that the troopers be sent there on a full-time basis. So Myles used a different tactic. He started mass picketing twenty-four hours a day, which meant the troopers had to work on shifts around the clock. They didn't care for this too much, much preferring the girls and the banjos. Since they were all staying at the same hotel, one of them came over to Myles one morning.

" Look," he said, " this getting up at 4 A.M. is a damned nuisance. Why don't we all get together and arrange a later opening time so we can all sleep? "

" Okay," Myles said. " Just so nobody brings scabs in earlier."

Of course the company couldn't keep to the agreement. They double-crossed both the union and the highway patrol and brought in a load of scabs at 4 A.M. So everybody had to start getting up again, with all-night picketing the order of the day. Myles also added another gimmick.

His phone was being tapped, so he arranged with a stooge in South Carolina to call him about an imaginary load of pickets who were to be shipped in by truck at 3 A.M. They'd haggle about the price of gas and other practical details to make it all sound realistic. Three nights in a row the fuzz roared off at 2:30 to intercept a truck that never came. The fourth night they didn't go, so the next night Myles had a real truckload of pickets shipped in. After this the cops were back to 2:30 again.

The obvious next step was government by injunction. The pickets were enjoined from coming close enough to company property to prevent scabs from entering the plant. Myles had an answer for that one too. He got a boy to go out and blow a bugle every morning at 4 A.M., waking up strikers for the picket line and incidentally all the rest of the town, including the scabs, who were thus aided to arrive at work sleepy and inefficient. The kid was finally hauled in for breach of the peace.

The oldest and most respectable lawyer in town, who had never shown any interest in the union, volunteered to take the case. Myles asked him why he was interested, and was told to come to the trial and see.

The old man put the kid on the stand and elicited testimony that made it perfectly clear that the boy had been disturbing the citizenry on Myles's instructions.

" Who told you to blow it? " the lawyer asked.

" Mr. Horton did. He told me to wake everybody up, to get the people out. He told me to blow that bugle so it would wake up all the union people, but to blow it so it wouldn't wake up the other people."

" Now, how did you do that? "

" Well, I never did quite understand how, but that's what he told me to do."

The lawyer then addressed the court.

"It's a terrible thing," he said, "to have noise disturbing people at four in the morning. For years the company has been blowing a whistle at five o'clock — a whistle that woke people who never expected to work in their plant. It's been waking everybody up in this town for twenty years, been waking up everybody in the county for ten miles around for twenty years. Now, I submit that this boy is guilty of waking people up with this bugle, but if he is guilty, the company is guilty, and I think you ought to fine them in proportion to the number of people they woke up."

The case was dismissed.

Then there's the case of the enthusiastic Indian. There are a lot of Indians in those parts, Croatans, who are reputed to be descendants of Sir Walter Raleigh, have English names, and have never spoken any language but English. In the thirties they were making their living as farmhands, mill-workers, and moonshiners.

One day about fifteen strikers, in opposition to Myles's better judgment, decided to invade the plant and chase out the scabs. They did, a hundred and fifty of them who came back to work later in the morning, and the cops moved in to arrest the strikers for trespassing, an offense of which they were clearly guilty. The enthusiastic Indian whacked a lieutenant in the jaw and knocked him in a double flip all the way down the mill stairs. They were all arrested for trespassing, a minor offense, with one extra charge against a person unknown for interfering with an officer, a serious charge.

Next day in court the lieutenant was asked if he could identify his assailant.

"Can't say that I can," he said. "So much was happening."

179

"Was it him?" the prosecution asked, pointing to the Indian.

"I can't be sure," the lieutenant said. "I couldn't testify."

Afterwards, in the hotel dining room, Myles went up to the lieutenant to thank him for his testimony.

"Hell," the cop said, rubbing his swollen jaw, "anybody who packs a wallop like that has my respect."

There's a large moral in this small story. Most of the troopers were country boys themselves. They were bought and owned by the state, which was owned by the mills, but their sympathies were generally with the strikers. In 1937, their parents were probably eking out a living by cropping or working in a mill somewhere. It's different now.

The leading moonshiner in town was also an Indian. He drove a big Packard, which everybody got out of the way of, including the cops. He was considered friendly but had never made any overtures to the strikers. One day he pulled up in front of the picket line and called Myles over.

"Horton," he said, "I want to talk to you. The company has hired four or five Indians to take you out in a swamp and lose you. What they don't know is that those are my boys. I've gotten them out of jail, they work at my still, and they take orders from me. I've told them I don't want anybody bothering you. I want them to get their money and then follow you around. You'll have bodyguards on company pay. I know you may think this is a little irregular, but you don't have much choice. You either trust me or get killed."

Myles trusted him, and he had a bodyguard for weeks, until the company realized their investment wasn't paying off.

It wasn't all fun and games. They tried intimidation. A car full of drunken gunmen hauled up in front of Myles's hotel one night. He'd been forewarned of it. He'd even been given a pistol, which he didn't know how to use, by a Holiness minister in Lumberton.

"Keep this, Brother Horton," the minister said. "You may need it."

Myles threw it in a bureau drawer and forgot about it until the gunmen showed up.

They yelled up at him from the street.

"Horton," they said, "come on down. We don't like organizers in this town."

Myles remembered the gun.

"Okay," he said, getting it out of the drawer, "I've got a deal to offer you. You outnumber me, and you're going to get me. But I'll get a couple of you before you do. So I think you fellows ought to organize, choose up and see who's the fellow I'm going to get first. I think you need a union."

There was dead silence in the car. Then it disappeared.

They also sent three hooded klansmen to the hotel to tell Myles he would be killed if he held a meeting that night. The killers showed up on schedule, mostly drunk, at a meeting where Myles had exhorted the strikers not to come armed. But the hill people, exercising a more ancient wisdom, took precautions. While Myles was talking about the Bill of Rights, the boys were all cocking pistols in their pockets, and a union leader standing behind Myles on the steps fished out a double-barrelled shotgun.

"You sons of bitches," he said, "if you don't get out of here I'm going to kill you."

The company thugs rapidly lost interest and disappeared.

Myles went to jail once when he refused separate bail. He was cited for contempt of court on another occasion, a charge that was dropped after the strike was won. The ministers got together one Sunday and all preached sermons against Horton and the strike. A committee of businessmen called on him and advised him that in the best interest of the local community he should leave town. Myles explained that there was a kind of degeneracy that set in when people had lived in an isolated community for generations, one that affected you physically. His people had lived in the Tennessee mountains since back before the revolutionary war, when Tennessee was still part of North Carolina, and he just didn't have the energy to leave town. As educated and informed people they would understand that. Somehow they didn't seem to.

Myles had the same trouble with relief they'd had in Grundy County. It was controlled by the company and the local administrator, like Mrs. Shivers of the Red Cross in Wilder, was a relative of a company official. It had been a long strike and the people were getting desperately hungry. Myles, as organizer, went to the relief office and asked for help. He offered to do most of their work for them, including the warehousing and distribution of food. They refused to certify the strikers.

This was becoming an old story, and Myles came up with another fine answer. He wired Harry Hopkins and Aubrey Williams in Washington asking them to put pressure on the state and county to get relief for the strikers. Washington wired back that the strikers were entitled to relief and that there was no reason why they shouldn't get it. This interchange went on for some time. Every time a telegram came Myles would read it to his nightly meetings.

These meetings were a marvelous feature of the strike. Everybody in town attended them — strikers, scabs, troopers, and company officials. It was the only entertainment available in Lumberton. They had singing and dancing and educational talks by Myles. This was where he gave most of his impromptu courses, including one in practical journalism where he made nightly predictions about what all the newspapers in the area would say the next day.

For three weeks he kept reading telegrams and explaining that relief was something the strikers had a legal right to. When he considered the indoctrination period was finished, he made a direct attack on local officials, naming names. He said some pretty strong things that didn't sit very well with the local bureaucrats. Next day he went back to the relief office and insisted that they deal with him on behalf of the union. The woman in charge refused but said she would deal with the strikers as individuals.

At the meeting that night Myles apologized to the strikers. He told them he had played square with them, but that he had failed because he hadn't realized that the relief office wouldn't deal with him as a representative of the union. Unwittingly he had led them to believe he could do something for them he couldn't do. From now on they'd have to do it themselves. The local brass went home certain that they had won a great victory.

Next morning, promptly at opening time, a thousand people showed up at the relief office. They shoved and pushed ahead of each other and in general caused a hell of a ruckus. Whenever a clerk would start to take an application, somebody else would shove in ahead and demand to be served first. They acted like individuals, all right — individuals in cahoots. They tramped so hard on the porch of the old building the office was housed in that the porch collapsed. This went on for several hours, until in desperation the officials called the police. But there was nothing the fuzz could do. The strikers were all there, as was their right, looking for their individual relief. And they sure weren't getting service.

When that didn't work, the relief administrators asked the union president if he couldn't do something.

" Hell, no," he said, " I'm an individual, I want my relief, I've got a family and I'm going to get it. You said you wanted to deal with us as individuals. Just take my application, will you, and get those folks ahead of me out of the way."

As a last resort they put in a call to Raleigh.

" You're supposed to deal with those people down there," the state office replied. " That's what we've been telling you. You've got to work out some way to handle them."

" But they've gone crazy. They all want to be treated as individuals."

" Do you want to deal with the union? "

" Well, no. But something went wrong somewhere. What do we do? "

While they were trying to settle on what to do, the strikers went out on the lawn and had a picnic of hamburgers and apples, supplied from Myles Horton's expense account. As the picnic was concluding, a delegation from the relief office came out to ask help from Myles.

" Not me," he said. " I'm not on relief, I don't need relief, and I don't have any interest in it. The CIO pays my salary and I have no intention of making an application."

And he walked away.

In a little while the cops came to dicker with him.

" I don't want any relief," Myles said. " You can't make people take relief if they don't want it. I'm not interested."

This time he went back to his hotel room.

Around four o'clock he got a phone call from an official of the State Relief Administration, presumably from Raleigh.

" You've got the wrong number,'" Myles said. " I don't

want any relief. I'm working down here and I get paid. There are a lot of other people who do want it. You might help them instead."

And he hung up.

In a minute the phone rang again.

"Listen," the voice said, "I'm not in Raleigh. I'm right here in this hotel and I've got to see you."

"I'm sorry, mister," Myles said, "you've got the wrong fellow. I can help you by telling you where the people are who want relief, but I don't want it myself."

"Now look," the voice said, "don't hang up on me again. I'm coming up."

The caller was a fat man with the jollity often wrongly attributed to people his size. He sat down on the bed and laughed until the tears came to his eyes.

"This is the funniest thing I ever heard," he said. "But it's also very embarrassing to the State Administrator. You've got us licked. What do you want?"

"We want relief, and we want it fast."

"I'm willing to bargain. I want you to organize this thing."

"Look," Myles said. "We wanted to do it that way all along and you wouldn't do it our way. Now you're going to have to pay us to do it. What will you give?"

"I'm prepared to pay," the man said. "What will be your price for taking care of this thing in an organized way and handling it?"

"Immediate relief commodities turned over to the union depot. We have a place here where we will distribute from, and we'll sign receipts for several tons of stuff. When you've done that, we'll talk to you."

"How much you want?"

"Oh, a couple of truckloads," Myles said. "Those moving vans. We've got people hungry. We want enough to keep them over for a while."

" I'll have four truckloads here in three hours. What do you want me to do with them? "

" Turn them over to the strike committee."

The man got on the phone.

" Release four trucks," he told Raleigh. " Yes, I said four. Get a receipt from the strike committee. That's what I said. No, that's all you get. Just unload and go on back. And I want that stuff here in less than three hours."

" Now," he said, turning to Myles, " can I meet with the committee? "

" Sure, though I doubt they'll talk to you until they see the food. They've been fooled too often."

So Myles called the committee and arranged for them to come in after the trucks were unloaded. An efficient system was quickly worked out. Fifty men at a time would go over to register and Raleigh would send over eight people to help out. They had them all registered in a couple of days. Meanwhile there was food until the regular relief began.

The outstanding feature of this strike was that Myles always had the establishment off balance. They never knew what was happening until it was all over. You can settle things pretty quickly once you've let them back themselves into a corner.

This is another strike that was won through government help, but of a different kind. Lumberton was the scene of the first collective bargaining election held by the NLRB in the South. But before this could happen the strike had to be lost. This is no paradox. Myles called the strike off, but he had a hell of a time doing it.

He had a meeting of about twenty-five of his best people and explained his strategy. They didn't have the strength now to win. Besides, with all the scabs the company had imported, the plant was starting to produce a little again. The TWU had won the NLRB election, 500–319 against the company union, and the mill was legally required to take the strikers back; the company had advertised asking their return. The thing to do was go back as a union, negotiate a contract while they were working, and keep their jobs secure. After an all-night session, the committee reluctantly agreed.

A mass meeting of the strikers Sunday night was something like a revival meeting where the preacher has just admitted he doesn't believe in God. Pandemonium broke loose. These people had been out for months and they had developed a sense of solidarity. They broke down and cried. Myles had promised to stick with them, they were going to lick the company, they believed in the union, they believed in themselves, they believed in Myles and now he was telling them they had to go back.

He finally got across the idea that they were going back as a union, so next morning, before the scabs arrived, they all went in and took over their old jobs. When the strikebreakers got there, there weren't any jobs to be had. The company, thinking with its usual ponderousness, told the union people they'd have to leave. They refused. The jobs were legally theirs.

A sitdown strike was forbidden by North Carolina law, but there were other possibilities. After they'd been back at work for a while, little things began to go wrong. A cotton mill is a pretty delicate operation; if everything doesn't flow evenly along the line, there's trouble. Bad cotton can get mixed in with the good, and the strings break. The weavers, the most skilled labor in the mill, may have a breakdown. The possibilities are infinite, and the union used them.

The foreman was up to his neck in trouble. Every time he thought he had things straightened out something else would happen, and the management was on his neck. So he went to the union leaders and asked what was wrong. It's the non-union men who make up 30 percent of the workers, they explained. The union people just didn't have any enthusiasm for working with people who didn't go along with them when times were tough. The company, ignoring an obvious solution like expediting a contract, put up a quota chart with an honor roll for people who made their quotas.

The trouble was that only union people ever made their quotas. The non-union people were good workers, but they never got any cooperation. Their cotton wasn't there, or their thread wasn't, or if it was, the next person who was supposed to take off was never quite ready. When a non-union machine broke down, the loom-fixers went to work dutifully when the foreman told them to, but they never could seem to find the trouble. They were careful to do no damage to the machinery, but it took them a hell of a long time to make repairs and they usually managed to get the machine spread all around while they were looking for the trouble. Repairs on union machines went like clockwork and there were never any bottlenecks with their materials.

After about a week the foreman got the point.

"What do you guys want?" he said.

"A contract. We're not going out on strike, we're not going to sit down, and we aren't going to damage anything, we aren't going to threaten the non-union men. But our hearts aren't in it when we can't get a contract. Until we do, you're not going to get any production."

The foreman, whose job depended on production, sided with the men, and management, whose profits depended on them, reluctantly agreed. Myles had to call the union out for only one day, just to remind management it could still be done. Production rose immediately.

There were further problems. After the contract was signed, there were negotiations about details — what group should get what increase and the like. When they reached the Negroes, the plant manager said, " Well, I understand how you feel about it, but I'm a Republican. These colored people work on my plantations out here and they work in my mill — they're good boys and I think we ought to do something for them."

" Naw," Myles said, " nothing special. I think they'll be satisfied with the minimum."

The manager almost had apoplexy.

" The *minimum!* " he screamed. " That more than triples their wages, and it cuts their hours down from sixty to forty hours. You don't mean to say you expect me to pay them $12.00? "

" Look at the contract," Myles said. " That's what it says. Twelve dollars is the minimum wage. You signed it."

" I won't do it," he said.

" Okay," said Myles, " don't. Just one thing, though. If you fire a single Negro, if there isn't a $12 check for every Negro next week, we'll close your plant down tighter than a drum. I don't want to argue with you. I'll go over and call them out right now if you want me to. Maybe it'll save us all a lot of time."

" Now wait a minute," the manager said. " Don't do that. I'll live up to the contract. But it's not right just the same."

Payday came, and the Jim Crow windows opened up. There was a big line at the white window. As each got his envelope he opened it on the spot to make sure his raise was there. It invariably was. The Negroes hung back. Twelve dollars was too much to hope for. Up to now their high man had been getting $9, the rest $6 and $4 — for a sixty- to seventy-hour week. This week they had worked only forty hours.

Finally they edged up to the colored window and got their envelopes, but they didn't open them. Myles was sitting under a tree across the street, just seeing what went on, and they came across the road in his direction. They got in a little huddle, and finally one of them opened his envelope. It was $12.00. They were all $12.00. Spontaneously, their faces alight, they came over to Myles. That was when he burst out crying. The precise thing one of them said to him was: "Thank you for all the colored folks. Ain't no white man ever done nothing like that for niggers in North Carolina."

It was a fitting climax to the original difficulties Myles had in getting them into the union. This was a white man's town, Myles was a white organizer, and it had to be a white man's union. They didn't trust him, and Myles saw no reason why they should. So he waited until he had most of the white strikers signed up and then began to ask who was the leader of the Negroes. Finally one Negro said, "You want to see the he-coon. I'll take you to him tomorrow."

The he-coon, the man who ran the show, looked at Myles impassively while Myles explained that the union was for everybody, that he had always emphasized the fact that he wanted all the Negroes in, and that there was no distinction between whites and Negroes, anymore than there was between men and women. These were brave words, but in a white town that had a nine o'clock curfew for Negroes, where a Negro found in town fifteen minutes after the curfew whistle would be thrown in jail for the night, the he-coon could hardly be expected to believe them. Obviously he didn't. He didn't say anything; just sat there expressionless.

"Look," Myles said. "I know you don't believe me. If I were in your place I wouldn't trust me either. But I've got a simple proposition for you. I've got most of the white people signed up, and I'll be glad to show you their membership cards. We may have a strike, but we're going to get a contract. Now if we get a contract and you're in the union, your interests will be protected as union members. It won't cost you a nickel to join. I want to give you some membership cards and I want you to get people signed up. Think it over and talk about it with your people."

Next day the he-coon came around. "Give me the cards," he said. It wasn't that he trusted Myles yet; he just had it figured that he had nothing to lose, and that Negroes stood a better chance of winning as union members than as outsiders. When the strike came, the Negroes were the best pickets on the line, lively, enthusiastic, always helping to keep everybody's spirits up. And in the first organizational meeting after the contract was in force, Negroes were accepted without question. You have to know the South in the thirties to understand what a blockbuster that one is. Only Highlander could have done it.

Myles's philosophy of organizing was part of Highlander's whole approach to any problem: get the people together and help them start solving their problems. His first step with a new union was to set up committees and begin turning responsibility over to them. He'd offer ideas and guidance where it was necessary, but he strove constantly to have the people take over. He'd spend hours helping a committee reach a decision on something he could have done himself in fifteen minutes. His philosophy was that the worst thing an organizer could do was to get the workers to depend on him for instructions. Then they had simply substituted the organizer for the boss, and when the organizer left town he did not leave behind him a union capable of fending for itself or reaching its own decision. The result, one way or another, was bound, in the long run, to be disaster.

Myles's approach — Highlander's approach — worked. In fact, it worked too well for a union which, as early as 1937 and with only a foothold established in the South, was already becoming stratified. It took Myles a while to realize this. Among the first things that convinced him was the expense account problem.

One of his organizational techniques was to provide things that helped people carry out group action, like the hamburgers and apples for the picnic outside the relief office, or a truckload of salted fish he bought one day when a much publicized fishing expedition produced only one small fish. He knew that families were depending on fish for supper that night. One way or another, he was determined to provide it.

When the union refused to provide funds direct for such items, Myles simply put them on his expense account. As a result, he regularly had the highest expense accounts in the area. Union officials, already beginning to act like businessmen, protested.

" All right," Myles said, " I'll cut it down if you don't want to get any organizing done. But I'll make you a proposition. You match the dollars you give me against those you give anybody else, and the number of dues-paying members I'll bring in against those anybody else does. I'll guarantee to at least equal anybody else in the country." They accepted the challenge and both the union and Myles kept records. It turned out that Myles was doing a better job than any other

CIO organizer in the South. This quieted things temporarily, but it didn't sit well with the union brass.

I can't leave expense accounts without telling Strictland's story. Strictland was a fifty-year-old textile worker who had formerly lived in Lumberton and who came in to help Myles organize. He was a delightful character who couldn't write, though he could read a little, and he had a hell of a time with his expense accounts, even though he regularly had the least expenses of any organizer in the region. Myles used to help him with them in addition to writing letters to his wife and his letters to the paper.

One of his big troubles was vouchers. It was just too much trouble, Strictland felt, to get receipts for everything he did. The way he looked at it, if the union trusted you to organize for them they ought to trust you to turn in an honest expense account. The union office didn't see it that way and kept the pressure on for vouchers. Strictland was fuming. One day he discovered, on the mantle of his home, a yellowed shoe box into which they had been throwing receipts — light receipts, water receipts, hospital receipts, baby registration receipts, coffin receipts, the whole business of family living. He brought them in and they wrapped them up and sent them to New York, along with a note that Strictland dictated to Myles.

"Here are your receipts," it said. "When you've used them up, let me know and I'll get you some more."

The union's private response is not recorded, but Strictland kept on organizing. Myles was a different kind of problem.

The expense accounts were only a pretext. The real trouble was that his people were too damned democratic. They ran their own affairs and weren't interested in taking orders from anybody, including the union. They organized politically and elected a sheriff, a key figure in any small Southern milltown. They were definitely not the docile, dues-paying members the union now wanted, members who would be content to follow a line handed down from the top.

Something had to be done about Horton. They couldn't put up with him and it would be embarrassing to fire such a successful organizer. So they kicked him upstairs, raised his salary from $30 to $70 and called him State Organizer, an administrative position in which he was carefully shielded from any actual organizing. When Myles realized what was happening, he quit and went back to Highlander.

But the Lumberton story was not yet finished. The TWU sent in a new organizer who tried to follow the union line and hand down instructions from the top. The workers didn't take to it. They were used to running their own affairs, in the Highlander fashion. They told the organizer so many times that " that's not the way Myles would have done it " that he could have cheerfully strangled Horton. Meanwhile, the company, seeing its opportunity, moved in. " Why don't you have a union of your own," they said, " so you can make your own decisions? You don't have to take orders from those Yankees up in New York. We'll guarantee to recognize you."

The people wavered, and the organizer panicked. In desperation the union called Myles and asked him to go down and see what he could do about it. " I can only go for a couple of days," he said, " but I'll do it." It happened that John Pate, president of the Lumberton local, was then a student at Highlander, having been sent up to try to learn something about how to fight the company union. The day before the workshop ended, he and Myles set out for Lumberton.

On the way they stopped at the regional office, where

Myles demanded full authority and a blank check for anything he wanted to do. He got it. He made these demands for two reasons: because he couldn't do a job if he weren't running the show and because he wanted the present organizer to get a wire saying Horton was taking over. There couldn't be a quicker way to get the word around. When he got to town he was expected — and welcomed, by the people if not by the organizer.

He spent the rest of the morning and early afternoon riding around in a car decked with posters announcing a meeting that evening, stopping to talk to everybody and giving them the word. He didn't say they were going to have a strike, but he didn't contradict the rumor either. The strongest group in the union was the afternoon shift of weavers. He got together with them in advance and they called a quick strike in the union's strongest spot and the company's weakest. You can't make cloth without weavers, and you can't run a mill without them either, even one shift of them. The thread piles up and you've got a hell of a mess.

By six o'clock the company had agreed to meet with the union committee and accept their demands. Myles left town next morning, his mission accomplished. All he had done was renew the workers' confidence in themselves and demonstrate to them that their union, not a company union, could do the job. The Lumberton local was back in business and stayed that way.

Highlander continued labor education on all kinds of fronts — in workshops which trained leadership, both at the school and in local communities; on the action front in strikes, though Myles had given up organizing; and in various sorts of community organization. For sheer entertainment, my favorite among the latter is the tobacco spitting contest at the Union Label Fair held in La Follette, Tennessee, in 1937. The event was reported this way in the La Follette *Press*, June 22, 1937:

TOBACCO SPITTING CONTEST

Bob Yoder won a closely contested union tobacco spitting contest at La Follette today with a reach of twelve feet one inch. The contest was part of a Union Label Fair, a feature of the Workers Education Rally which the Highlander Folk School is holding for the Amalgamated Clothing Workers of America from May 29th to July 5th.

Five hundred people crowded the union hall to see the exhibits of union label goods and to take part in the drawings of union label articles donated by local merchants.

The tobacco spitting contest drew old time miners, lumber workers, and other grey bearded mountaineers from neighboring coves and settlements of Campbell County. Old timers and youngsters stepped up to the chalk line for honors. It was a serious business for the contestants, for mountain men have been known to commit suicide for sheer embarrassment when they missed a knot hole at twenty-five feet. But the contest provided great merriment for the hundreds of spectators who lined the sidewalks of the town and cheered their favorites.

Bill Young, a sixteen year old stripling from Scaptown, led the field in the first trials, but experience finally won the day when Bill failed to maintain the terrific pace he set at the start. The final score of the Campbell County championship Tobacco Spitting Contest was Bob Yoder, first, with twelve feet one inch; Charlie Brown, second, with eleven feet nine inches; Bill Young, third, with eleven feet four inches; and Adam Young, fourth, with a flat eleven feet.

A group of old timers judged the spitters on a basis of distance and form. To have good form, they explained, was to keep the wad together and to give a good arch to it so as to catch the glint of the sun and so give off the beautiful amber glint that brings joy to the heart of the real old time tobacco spitter.

Another feature of the Union Label Fair was an initiation of foxhound "music" by M. K. McKinney of Caryville, and a leader of a newly organized group of lumber workers at Duff, Tennessee. McKinney threw back his great shaggy head and produced some real "music" that old timers declared was perfect.

The Workers Education Rally will close with a huge labor Fourth of July Labor Rally on July 5th. The program is under the direction of four members of the Highlander Folk School staff.

If you think this was just fun and games, you couldn't be more wrong. The Union Label Fair, of which the spitting contest was a feature, was an integral part of Highlander's first major extension program.

La Follette, a town of 2500 in 1937, lies in the mountains of northeast Tennessee in the heart of the TVA country, twenty miles north of Norris. Two shirt factories there employed about a thousand women and girls, most of whom commuted from mountain communities within a twenty-mile radius, some of them paying twenty-five cents a day taxi fare. Wages had been low, about a dollar a day. The highest paid girl in the pressing room made $12 a week for a day which usually began at 5:45 A.M. and ended at 5 P.M. In January, 1937, the workers struck. The organizer was a former Highlander student who formed a local of the Amalgamated Clothing Workers of America. The strike was won and union recognition and a wage raise were granted.

The problem now was to accomplish the kind of thing Myles had worked at in Lumberton — to help a thousand people who had absolutely no experience in the labor movement to become active and responsible union members. His Highlander training had taught the organizer that unless he accomplished this the union would not hold together in times of real stress. Accordingly he called on Highlander for help. The school had already placed its facilities at the disposal of the TWOC for the duration of the organizing drive; here was an opportunity to lend further help and to try out Highlander techniques in the field in a full-scale extension program. It was decided to cancel that year's summer session and hold a five-week educational rally in La Follette instead.

Highlander arrived at just the right time. The union was experiencing its first letdown. The workers had won the strike and a wage raise, and they had a union. But the union wasn't doing anything, and employers were already beginning the tactics we have seen in Lumberton. The clarinets and bombardons were already tuning up for a performance of " You Don't Need a Union." The problem therefore was to interest the people, to get them to participate in the rally and then in the union's affairs. What was called for was a mixture of recreation and education — a task which fitted precisely into Highlander's pattern but which the school had never tried before under these circumstances.

They went at it with characteristic ingenuity. Classes were held afternoons and evenings in La Follette and the neighboring town of Caryville. There were ball games, ping-pong tournaments, picnics and, always, singing. The workers got out their own mimeographed newspaper, " The Shirt Tale." The union hall was spruced up with colorful charts, posters, and photographs. A library was set up, and 200 books and pamphlets were displayed in the windows. The union hall thus became the town's only library except for the corner drugstore. In these more attractive surroundings workers discussed topics like Why We Need the Union, How the Union Works, The CIO: an Industrial Union, The Clothing Industry, and Social Security.

The Union Label Fair was a smash hit. Union products were displayed and offered as prizes; for example, the Brown and Williamson Company in Louisville donated eighty pounds of tobacco. At the height of the spitting contest crowds so clogged the streets that traffic to Jellico, twenty miles to the north, was practically halted.

The big closing event was the Fourth of July Labor Celebration. Led by the Jellico High School Band, locals of the United Mine Workers, the United Lumber Workers, the Workers Alliance, and the Amalgamated Clothing Workers of America paraded to the fairgrounds. It was like a Tennessee mountain equivalent of *Meistersinger*, Act III. The Prize Song was speeches by AFL and CIO representatives, and the chorus was shouts from the audience: "AFL or CIO, we got to get together." As usual, the people were way ahead of the brass. Over 4,000 (in a town of 2500) attended the festivities, which concluded with a hog-calling contest (results disputed), a ball game, fireworks, and dancing in the streets. La Follette had never had it so good.

Thus ended Highlander's first major effort at an extension program. It was an unqualified success. A substantial number of union members became actively engaged in leadership activities, and all the membership had a new sense of solidarity and a pride in the new prestige in the community which the rally had brought them. However, there were obvious limitations from Highlander's point of view. The whole staff was involved at La Follette, and education at the school was simply shut down. Various experiments were undertaken which involved sending out one staff member into a specific situation: to Alcoa, Tennessee, for six week's work with an Aluminum Workers local, to New Orleans for a full year's work with all the unions in the area. Finally the pattern which was to continue for some years evolved: leadership classes in local communities, much like those conducted at the school itself, requested and financed by the unions.

Highlander continued active in strikes all over the South;

you will remember that it was from a tobacco workers' strike in the forties that " We Shall Overcome " developed. Zilphia brought music to the whole area. The program of leadership workshops, both at Highlander and throughout the South, benefiting from strong union support and a solid basis of experience, grew steadily and reached a greater variety of workers. For example, during the third CIO leadership school held at Highlander in May, 1946, there were Texas oil workers, Alabama shipyard and hosiery workers and Tennessee textile workers. Georgia furniture workers and many others gathered at the school. All these were people sent by their own unions to acquire tools which they could use in their own locals. Always with reference to immediate problems, they studied public speaking, parliamentary law, labor history, organizing methods, and collective bargaining. What was studied varied from workshop to workshop and from situation to situation, but this is fairly typical.

Though the curriculum always varied to meet specific needs, the organization of Highlander workshops soon developed, on the basis of experience, into a more or less standard pattern, one you could extrapolate from its philosophy. For example, the fall term that same year, 1946, included the election of a Student Council which would run the two-week course in leadership training. Students and staff alike participated in the Council (though only students held office) which represented a student body of seventeen CIO members from five Southern states, including four women and two Negroes.

After everybody had settled in, the term officially opened with a get-acquainted meeting the first night. Everybody introduced himself, both staff members and students; the students were asked to say a little about their unions and how they happened to join them. Elia Kazan's movie, *People of the Cumberland,* in which Highlander is the protagonist, was shown. Myles spoke briefly about the school, its early struggles, and its purpose and policies, including absolute nondiscrimination. The second night, after the students had had a chance to get acquainted, the Council was elected; even though they were to hold office for only two weeks, they took their responsibilities seriously. Next morning they were conferring with Myles about the curriculum.

We don't see we need that study period mid-morning, they said. Let's face it: nobody uses it. Didn't they need a breather in the middle of the morning? The schedule was pretty full. Well, a fifteen-minute recess, maybe, but nobody wanted a study period. But they hadn't had any assignments yet, Myles pointed out, and tomorrow they would. This was about the only time they could do them. Why didn't they wait a couple of days to make up their minds? If they still wanted to dispense with the study period, well, they were in charge.

The study periods were continued, but only because the students soon came to realize that they needed them. That was the Highlander way. Let them find out for themselves and reach their own decisions.

The focus in this session was on discrimination. Cooperative living and shared responsibility helped to break down barriers, as did recreation programs: hiking, swimming, volley ball. Rigorous classes had the same effect: Leadership Training, Economics, and Current Events pointed up the fact that discrimination was costly, that it was part of the divide and conquer tactic that kept workers at a constant disadvantage. Discussion grew so heated that a special evening program was devoted to discrimination. At the end of the term some of the white students admitted that they had been disturbed by having Negroes in the class but that they now felt differently about it.

They even learned how to deal with reverse discrimination. One day in Economics class, a Negro student was asked if a salesman could lower the price of an expensive article if he were offered only half the price. The idea of the question was to develop some insight into markups. "Sure," the Negro student replied, "if he's a Jew." Laughter was followed by embarrassed silence. After the class a white student complained to the term director that such remarks were contrary to the CIO policy of nondiscrimination.

It was the only such incident of the term. That Sunday one of the Negro students, a lay minister, preached the sermon and a white textile worker led the singing. This was brotherhood in action, and the students were genuinely moved. Integration was new to them, but it was taking.

The banquet which climaxed the term revealed an entirely different gathering than the one that had come there only two weeks before. They were a group now, and proud of it. Their diplomas represented a real accomplishment. The banquet committee went all out in decorating the dining room in a United Nations motif and transforming the Reading Room into a Cowboy Bar where cokes and orange pop were served at tables covered with red-checkered cloths. The last issue of the student newspaper was distributed. The skits revealed an astonishing amount of talent and reminded all these potential leaders that the same kind of resources could be tapped in their local unions. When the student body president and the term director gave farewell speeches, it was an emotional time.

Here's the schedule they went through to achieve this solidarity:

6:30		Reveille
7:00		Breakfast
7:30–	8:30	Work Period
9:00–12:00		Three 45-minute classes and one study period
12:30		Lunch
1:00–	2:00	Work Period
2:00–	3:30	Two 45-minute classes
3:30–	4:00	Committee meetings
4:00–	6:00	Recreation
6:00		Dinner
6:30–	8:00	Practice speeches and singing
8:00–	9:15	Evening Program
9:15–10:30		Free time; entertainment generally provided by the recreation committee for those who desired it.

Regardless of the group, the course, or the immediate problems, this became the general pattern of Highlander workshops. Democracy worked at Highlander partly because staff and students worked too. Almost without exception, workers went back to their local unions with an obvious increase in efficiency, understanding, and enthusiasm, and for this reason the unions kept sending new students. As a result, thousands of union workers in the South attended Highlander classes, and the influence of this little old school in Monteagle extended to a degree that General Ab Sloan lacked even a modicum of the imagination necessary to conjure up.

In an interview with Stanley Elam (*Phi Delta Kappan,* May, 1966), Myles Horton divides the typical Highlander workshop into three parts. The first is having people come up with their own problems; the second is helping them dis-

A break between classes at a Highlander workshop. Myles Horton in the center. PHOTO BY EARL WILLIMETZ.

cover that they have answers themselves which cannot be promulgated from on high or from the outside; the third is exploring what they will do after they get back home. Myles put it this way: "My position is that whatever Highlander has been able to do in changing people and helping them achieve a certain feeling of dignity comes from the fact that we deal with people who come with problems. We don't justify our existence on the basis of what happens in a week or month at Highlander. The educational process has started long before they come, and continues after they leave." This format spans every activity in which Highlander has been engaged.

The most interesting of Highlander's cooperative ventures with unions in the field of labor education was its work in 1952–1953 with the United Packing Workers of America, a union still sufficiently militant, even in these latter days, to reject the CIO's all-out endorsement of American intervention in Vietnam and come out for negotiation instead of bombs. With Ralph Helstein, UPWA president, a militant and democratic unionist, Myles worked out a proposal under which Highlander was to undertake leadership training at the local level and Myles was to become educational director of the union. The arrangement was subsequently approved both by the union's executive committee and by Highlander's executive council.

At first all went well. Things proceeded along the Highlander plan of education for independent and democratic action. As Myles reported in late 1952:

In everything undertaken our aim has been to train people to do things for themselves. We have stayed in the background. Our efforts have been devoted to setting up a program that once in operation can move fairly rapidly towards activating the locals and developing local leaders. Immediate and limited results have been subordinated to the less spectacular job of taking the program of the UPWA directly and consistently to the stewards and through them to the membership.

Our conviction has grown that most of the problems must be solved in the districts where those responsible are in a position to know the situation and to follow through. Also, that it is imperative for us to reach deeper into the membership with a continuing program than has been heretofore.

However, trouble was already developing. Vice President A. T. Stephens, a strict believer in "we'll tell 'em and you make 'em do it," was, as personnel director, in charge of all staff except the five men and women working under Myles in the educational program. In January, 1953, he proposed that the educational staff be replaced by program coordinators who met his approval, line officials in the chain of command under him. "There is going to be a shift from straight education to program implementation," he wrote, adding that there was no place for Horton's people in the new program and that it was a waste of union funds to train local members to lead discussions.

Once again the Highlander program was succeeding all too well, from the point of view of a unionist who wanted to control things from the top. Free discussion in the locals was the last thing Stephens wanted.

Myles refused to work with Stephens but promised Helstein to stay on in the hope that the education program could be salvaged. The climax came at a UPWA staff school held at Highlander in March, a session which Myles and Helstein had hoped would provide a forum for realignment. Things went exactly contrary to their hopes. All plans for the school were made without consulting Myles, on the grounds that it was being run by the UPWA coordinators, not the education department. Although he was both education director of the union and director of Highlander, he had to insist before he was permitted to sit in. The meetings were conducted so undemocratically that he felt compelled to demand that people who disagreed with Stephens be permitted to say their piece, pointing out that freedom of discussion was a basic principle at Highlander. Even for this purpose he had difficulty in getting the floor.

On the last day of the conference, Myles sent in his resignation to President Helstein. "The Highlander Executive Council," he wrote, "gave me permission to continue with the UPWA until September, provided that our policies and methods continued to be similar. It is now my feeling that the present setup does not provide adequate opportunity for carrying out the program originally envisioned. I am resigning as educational director at the end of the month." He went ahead to say that he was still vitally interested in the welfare of the union, but felt he could do more good working at Highlander.

For all practical purposes, this marked the end of Highlander's primary emphasis on labor education. The school stood ready to give, and continued to give, assistance to any union which requested its services. But it had now become clear that the direction of the American labor movement as a whole was away from the grass roots democracy whose encouragement was Highlander's reason for being. Perhaps there wasn't enough for the workers to fight for any more, no real decisions for the local unions to make. Strikes, planned and implemented on the national level, were only another tool in the regular rounds of national wage negotiations. It's a little futile to try to encourage a fight for democracy for people who are satisfied without it.

Besides, another crisis loomed on the horizon, one where democracy was to be of the essence. This was in the area of civil rights, of the integration which had always been not only a primary article in Highlander's credo but an unvarying staple of its practice. To what would come to be known as the Freedom Movement, Highlander now turned its major attention.

CHAPTER FIVE

The Freedom Movement

━━✺━━━✺━━━✺━━━✺━━━✺━━━✺━━━✺━━━✺━━

From the beginning, Highlander has been flatly opposed to any kind of discrimination. This philosophy has applied not only to race, but to sex, religion, and politics. Only those who did not agree with Highlander's completely democratic principles were not welcome, on the grounds that they could neither profit by the school nor help it. We have seen how Vice-President Stephens' blatant disregard of democratic procedures led to Highlander's severing official connections with the UPWA.

As we have also noted, Dr. Charles Johnson, in the school's first days, became the first Negro to spend the night in the modern history of the mountain. Highlander regularly brought in Negro lecturers as participants in workshops and worked through every means at its command toward an integrated student body. However, it was not until 1944 that the first integrated workshop was held at the school. The reason for this was neither reluctance on Highlander's part nor a concern about the acceptance of Negro students by the community. (As early as 1935 the interracial All Southern Conference for Human Rights, which had been chased out of Chattanooga by bigots, had been held at Highlander with the express approval of the neighbors, who said: " This is your home. Hold your meeting and we'll see they don't bother you.") It was a well-known fact that negroes frequently came as members of the staff; most people in the community, who had come to trust Highlander after the early community activities described in Chapter II, were perfectly willing to accept this. Those who did not, and who would oppose Negro students, were bitterly against Highlander anyway.

The reason for the delay was timidity on the part of the unions. Since Highlander had early become a labor school, it had committed itself to accepting only those students nominated and sent by the unions. At last, in 1944, the United Automobile Workers, faced with the reality of a large and growing negro membership, decided to take the risk and accepted the invitation Highlander had been issuing since 1940, to set up a one-week integrated workshop. The session was a success. Against the advice of friends who urged against moving too fast, Highlander moved quickly to set up a month-long session. Despite dire predictions that white union members would quit coming to the school and that locals would send students once but never again, this too was a success. Highlander was launched on a completely integrated program which was to lead to a rapid expansion of its activities. By 1947 it was carrying out the fullest program in its history, with enrollments swelled not only by the admission of Negroes but by a tremendous increase in white students. Unions were sending workers, many of them not officers but rank and file members who had showed leadership potential, because the Highlander program *worked*. They were sending negroes because that worked too.

For example, one local which had originally opposed the new interracial policy continued to send students despite its

Summer camp at Highlander. PHOTO BY IDA BERMAN.

objections to the program. In 1946, the president of the local wrote the school:

> We plan to send four people, if we can find that many suitable ones. I set up a committee to work with the Executive Board to select these people. It's pretty had to get good people who will accept. . . . We don't dare not to tell them that there will be Negro students and some of them shy away at that. . . . I think we can get four that will be as good or better along this line as X was.

By 1947 this local had sent nineteen students to the school. Even more significantly, it sent Negro as well as white students in this year. Highlander's experience had brought into serious question the easy assumption that the Southern white worker will not associate with Negroes.

To say that Highlander was successful does not mean that it came easy. Long-ingrained prejudices are not easy to uproot. Also many unions were at first reluctant to tell students that the course would be integrated or failed to point out exactly what integration at Highlander actually meant. Integration at Highlander meant having classes together, working together, eating together, and playing together. It meant accepting each other as people. In the early days of the program a number of students reacted quite violently to this totally unfamiliar situation.

The previously mentioned 1946 CIO summer term was a particularly intense example of the problem. Five students had arrived with no understanding of the full implications of Highlander's interracial policy, and they made trouble. They could voice their disapproval in Student Council meetings, and did, but this didn't satisfy them. Several of them threatened to go home if Negroes were not segregated at meals. If the classes had not been so stimulating, they would probably have left before.

The staff pointed out that there were half a dozen tables in the dining room and no assigned seats. No one was forcing anyone to eat at the same table with the Negroes if they didn't want to. The staff also pushed hard for the CIO's official nondiscrimination policy and a CIO representative talked about the damage prejudice had done in the South. All classes managed to get around to the problem of discrimination. In the parliamentary law class Negroes and whites alternated as chairmen. All student committees were interracial. A Negro speaker from a local cooperative gave the students advice on the small co-op store they were operating to take care of their daily needs.

Tension gradually lessened until a new crisis arose in the third week. A Negro woman, a representative of the Urban League, was scheduled to address the student body. Several of the dissidents introduced a resolution in a Student Council meeting to deny her the right to speak. After an hour's talk by a CIO official who happened to be present, in which he pointed out the criminal stupidity of refusing to listen to anyone's views, the motion was withdrawn. But the trouble was not yet over.

A few days later, the film strip " Man in the Cage," a dramatization of the evils of prejudice, was shown. A lively discussion followed. The leader of the anti-Negro group warmly supported the Klan as a Christian organization which did all sorts of lovely things like looking after orphans, delivering Christmas packages, and protecting womanhood. His eloquent generalities were immediately punctured by a white student from Louisiana, who told about the Klan burning a cross on his lawn, when he was a child, because his

Participants in a typical Highlander workshop. PHOTO BY EMIL
WILLIMETZ.

family was Catholic. Most of the students were further impressed with a reading by Don West of poems from his *Clods of Southern Earth* which stressed the need for Negro and white workers to live and work together.

The climax came almost immediately. When President Truman denounced striking railway workers, including the Pullman Porters, a student committee composed a strong letter to the president. The Klan-admiring, Negro-hating leader of the dissidents flatly refused to sign it. That did it. Whatever influence he had left was completely gone, and the term concluded harmoniously, with the anti-Negro group, not the Negroes, as the outsiders.

This session was, for all practical purposes, the end of such incidents. Unions came to realize the importance of briefing their people properly, and Highlander's completely integrated program became simply a fact of life for all who attended the school, including a substantial number of Negroes who were to become key figures in the Freedom Movement in the years ahead.

The critical dates in the early years of the Freedom Movement were 1954, 1955, and 1960. Most of the South, conservative, liberal, and radical, was not ready for any of them. Highlander was ready for them all.

The first great breakthrough on the civil rights front was the Supreme Court decision, in March, 1954, which outlawed segregation in the schools, striking down the separate but equal doctrine which had been the justification for legal segregation in the separate but unequal schools of the South. The fact that by and large the decision took the conservative white South by surprise is only an indication of these people's lack of comprehension of a problem they have been diligent in proclaiming their understanding of. As a result it took some time for tokenism, their final and present answer,

Myles Horton, Eleanor Roosevelt, and James Stokely at a Citizenship and Integration Workshop, June, 1958.

to develop. Massive resistance, obviously foredoomed to failure, was attempted in a great many places on the local level, but only Virginia, despite noises, laws, and resolutions in Alabama, Georgia, South Carolina, and Mississippi, tried it on a state-wide basis — and lost.

As usual, Highlander was a year ahead. The UPWA workshops ended on March 13th, 1953; Myles's resignation, submitted at that time, became effective April. 1. On April 27–28 a special Executive Council Meeting approved a five-week workshop that summer on " The Supreme Court Decisions and the Public Schools." Seventy-one people attended, the majority of them Southern community leaders from nine states. They included ministers, farmers, industrial workers, college and high school teachers and students, YMCA secretaries, adult education leaders, and members of interracial, fraternal, and civic organizations. The workshop director was Paul Bennett, a Negro then doing graduate work at Howard University and a former Alabama high school teacher. A grant of $5000 from the Field Foundation made it possible to bring in discussion leaders and offer scholarships to community leaders who could not afford the course.

I cite these facts to illustrate the speed and efficiency with which Highlander, in its customary fashion, worked. The school's emphasis, as always, was on getting people to act for themselves, developing action at the grass roots. As its proposed follow-up stated:

Regardless of whether the Supreme Court ruling provides for complete integration or merely sets up another step in that direction, the pattern of integration adopted will be determined largely by the local communities. These will be political decisions, which means that the people in each community have it within their power to influence the school board to make the best possible decisions. A basic goal of this program, therefore, is to develop and execute a plan whereby community leaders in key Southern communities can be trained now to deal with whatever situation may arise after the Supreme Court decision.

The tone of the workshops was positive. The old recalcitrance was duly noted: Governor Jimmy Burns' statement in South Carolina that " if we have such a decision from the U.S. Supreme Court, we will give up the public school system as we know it "; Governor Gene Talmadge of Georgia's affirmation that " as long as I'm Governor, negroes won't go to the same school as whites "; and similar statements by Governor Wright of Mississippi, whose mantle Ross Barnett, to his confusion, was to inherit.

But this was only to set the temper of the times. Out of the sessions came a Guide to Action, " Working toward Integrated Public Schools in Your Own Community," along with a check-list; a film-strip, " The High Cost of Segregation," complete with a Guide and prepared by Highlander's film center under the direction of Emil Willimetz, another of Highlander's multifarious services we have not had previous occasion to mention; and concrete proposals, which were carried out, for a series of workshops at Highlander which would be extended into local communities, with the help of the Highlander staff, by leaders who had attended the Highlander courses, to be followed up by area conferences and other field work as needed.

All this almost a year before the Supreme Court decision was handed down.

The most important product, of course, was the training and inspiration received by the people attending the workshops. Here's a typical reaction:

I've had to attend many conferences and meetings in my time. I have to admit, with the amount of work I had to leave behind,

I was a little reluctant to come to what might prove to be " just another meeting." I am surely glad I came. I don't know when I have felt I gained so much that I could put into practical use. I have never met with a finer set of people. As soon as I get back, I am calling the first meeting. In fact, I have already written my son to pass on the word for this coming Tuesday.

In reporting the results of this workshop Highlander was able also to add that over 10,000 church, farm, labor, education, and community leaders had been trained at Highlander residence sessions and that an additional 15,000 to 20,000 leaders had been trained by the Highlander faculty in extension classes in every state in the South. That little old school had been kind of busy.

Summer workshops on public school integration were continued in 1954, 1955, 1956. As early as the summer of 1954, only a few months after the Court's decision had been handed down, Highlander was able to report the following results. In Knoxville, Highlander-trained people were sparking a citizens' committee on integration. In Oak Ridge, Highlander people were active in a group which achieved the distinction of making their community the first in Tennessee to announce integration of public school facilities. In Columbia, South Carolina, Highlander graduates, especially negroes, were organizing solidly in a highly hostile environment. In Tuskeegee, Alabama, the all-negro civic association was following the plan of political and economic action developed at the school the previous summer. Highlander students were forming active groups in Chattanooga, Nashville, and Atlanta.

But by 1956 the focus was changing from a special emphasis on desegregation of the schools to the fight for integration across the board which was later to become the Freedom Movement. New things were happening.

This is not the place for a sequential history of the Freedom Movement. Much has been written about it; the briefest and best comprehensive accunt is Anne Braden's incisive and penetrating analysis in *Monthly Review*, 17:3 (July–August, 1965). Nevertheless, some of its main events must be chronicled, both to illustrate Highlander's participation in them and to lay the groundwork for an analysis of what this revolution — and it *is* a revolution — means to the South and to America as a whole.

The next breakthrough began in December, 1955, in Montgomery, Alabama, when Mrs. Rosa Parks, a Negro seamstress, refused to give up her seat on a city bus to a white man. It wasn't that she was sitting in the "white" section in the front of the bus. She was in the first row of the Negro section. But when the white section filled up, the bus driver lifted the portable race-divider, a gimmick I used to be familiar with in New Orleans, from the seat ahead of Rosa to the seat behind her and ordered her to move. She was now in forbidden territory and the white man had a right to her seat.

She balked. For exactly what reason, she still doesn't know. She was tired, but she had often been tired before. The procedure wasn't new, either; she'd been living with it all her life. But on this day, somehow, she knew she'd had enough. She was not new at fighting segregation. She'd been doing that for a long time. Back in the thirties her husband had led a group which gathered secretly in their living room to raise funds for the Scottsboro boys. Subsequently she joined the NAACP, became the local secretary, and by patient, unflagging work helped hold the branch together.

But this was something new. Now she was publicly defying authority, an offense for which she knew she could be arrested. She was, and jailed as well, on the bus driver's initiative. In court, Judge John B. Scott, who ten years later was to remark to a *Newsweek* reporter that Rosa "would probably have been greatly disappointed had she been acquitted, for never has there been a more painless path to martyrdom," disposed of her case in five minutes with a conviction and a ten dollar fine. A routine affair, so he thought. He couldn't have been more wrong.

As usual, there was a bit of Highlander pre-history in this. Six months earlier, at a Highlander workshop on integration which was still primarily focused on the schools, Rosa Parks had joined other Negro participants from Montgomery in saying that there seemed to be little hope in their town. Montgomery Negroes, they feared, would never learn to stick together. They were too used to being fragmented, to living by the white man's whims. It's a mercy to us all that she was as wrong as the judge.

With her action having brought things to a head, Negro leaders in Montgomery issued a call for a bus boycott. They had no real idea whether the Negro community would support them. In fact, some of them later admitted that they were just as surprised as the city bosses when they saw the buses rolling empty through the Negro districts next day. They continued to roll empty for a year, until a court decision nullified the local bus segregation law. During that year fifty thousand Negroes had walked or set up their own jitney services. The court decision got the city fathers off the hook, since they could then pose as submitting to law and order rather than to rebellion, but there is no question that the case would never have been pushed through had it not been for a boycott that was hitting the city where it hurt — in its pocketbook.

Part of the success of the Montgomery boycott was a result of the happy conjunction of several remarkable people.

221

Rosa Parks was one of them. Quiet and retiring though she was — she never had ambitions to be a heroine — she had a will of steel. E. D. Nixon, President of the Union of Pullman Car Porters and the leader of the local NAACP, was another. Mrs. Parks called him from jail and he got the ball rolling in a hurry. With the help of a few other dedicated people he launched the boycott and guided it throughout. The other key figure was Martin Luther King, Jr., an unknown young minister who had recently come to Montgomery and who had been elected president of the Montgomery Improvement Association primarily because he had presence and was so new that he had not yet been absorbed into any of the factions that were tearing the organization apart.

Whether the Montgomery boycott would have succeeded without King is not a question that can be answered. There was almost unanimous support in the Negro community before he took over active leadership: hence the initial astonishing success. But there is no question that he played a major role in keeping the movement going through twelve agonizing months of threats, violence, bombings, and economic reprisals. Many Negroes lost their jobs, and those who didn't were seriously inconvenienced. When they got to work, they faced the unrelenting disapproval of their employers and the whole white community. But they refused to quit.

One of Martin Luther King's — I never write his name without reflecting on its appropriateness: he nailed his theses against a bus door instead of a church's, but they worked just the same — great talents was an enormous gift for oratory. This is immensely important in the South, especially but not solely among Negroes. Anyone trying to understand our region must begin by recognizing the importance of the oral and verbal tradition that is our heritage. In the nineteenth century, when debate and oratorical contests flourished and duels were verbal as well as lethal, it was an American tradition. Because of various leveling factors, including mass education and industrialization, the tradition died out very rapidly in the North and West. But it persisted in the South, mainly because this was a region which did not want to be leveled and which gloried in an isolation which the War Between the States had only intensified.

Rich and poor, white and Negro alike, were ravished by words. And still are, if they are *of* the South, not merely transplants. This, as I have noted before, is why it's writer's country. It's also why it's music country, a fact to which we shall shortly return. When Sam Irwin, for example, the shrewdest legal mind to reach the Senate floor via the North Carolina electorate in decades, puts on his oratorical clothes, his Northern colleagues generally assume he's going into old Sam's act. In fact he isn't. He's talking naturally, in the tradition he grew up in, and he's speaking a language which his electorate, until now overwhelmingly white, understands.

This has been even more true of the Negro community, where inadequate schooling has helped perpetuate the oral tradition full force. There is no place in America, even today, where you can hear preaching — and singing — of the caliber you will find in any Negro church in the South. It's pure soul-stirring emotion, the preaching and the music both, and into this tradition Martin Luther King spoke and was heard.

He had another advantage. He had something to say, something that made sense to the whole community, to the older people who recognized the preacher's ringing tones and to the young people who were in rebellion against the old safe traditions. "We will walk the streets of Montgomery until the walls of segregation are finally battered by the forces of justice," King proclaimed. "And when the history

books are written in future generations, the historians will
have to pause and say, ' There lived a great people — a black
people — who injected new meaning and dignity into the
veins of civilization.' "

Martin Luther King's genius was to sense people's aspira-
tions and to put these into words that both give them a
feeling of their own personal worth and move them to group
action. But beyond this he had another absolutely essential
and extremely rare quality — personal incorruptibility and
the courage to act on the beliefs he preached about. He
moved the Southern Negro, the listening white South, the nation, and the world, as his well-deserved Nobel Peace Prize
testifies.

Eventually we must consider the split between the cult of
personal leadership, the old Southern tradition exemplified
by SCLC (the Southern Christian Leadership Conference)
with King as the charismatic leader, and the commitment to
the leadership of the people themselves, a commitment now
swinging toward Black Power, exemplified by SNCC (the
Student Nonviolent Coordinating Committee). Before
reaching that point, however, I'd like to pause to pay a compliment to Reverend King, who was pilloried by the bigots,
as you will remember, for his attendance at Highlander's
twenty-fifth anniversary celebration a year later. Few men
these days, in his position, have been offered more tempta-
tions and blandishments. The bitch goddess took him up
on the mountain and showed him all he could own. King,
to the best of my knowledge, resisted this utterly, and remained himself, militant and unswerving for the truth. For
this we should all pay him homage. He paid for it with his
life, snuffed out by an assassin's bullet.

All over the South Negroes listened to Martin Luther King
and took heart. The Montgomery boycott had changed the

face of the South forever, but the idea was slow in spreading. Another bus boycott sprang up in Tallahassee, Florida, but White Citizens Councils multiplied far more rapidly than civil rights groups. The NAACP was outlawed in Alabama and Negro voting rights, pitifully inadequate as they were, were further restricted in most Southern states. The era of organized murder of civil rights workers began. Reverend George Lee is remembered as the hero of a current freedom song, but countless others, unnamed and unmentioned in the press, died by the same route. To our shame, it was only when whites also began to be killed that this campaign of murder became a national scandal. Most of those who have been shocked by the routine acquittal of killers by Southern juries fail to realize how many Negroes were murdered without even the posthumous compliment of a trial of their assassins.

"Somebody kilt?" the sheriff would say.

"Just a Nigger."

Case closed.

The fuse had been lit in Montgomery, but the big explosion was yet to come.

Meanwhile other things were happening.

In 1954 Highlander had a new student, Esau Jenkins from Johns Island, one of the Sea Islands lying just off Charleston, South Carolina. Esau had been born on the Island, the son of a carpenter. In his youth he first helped his father and then went to work on a farm for fifty cents a day. Already married and starting a family at eighteen, he knew he needed more money, so he began planting cotton with his father, later turning to truck farming. A couple of incidents from this period give an insight into his character.

He had to leave school after four years to go to work, but he studied hard the short time he was there and he learned

Esau Jenkins and Myles Horton on Johns Island, South Carolina.
PHOTO BY IDA BERMAN.

to figure. The first time they took a load of cotton in to sell, the white man figured what the cotton came to and gave them a price. Esau figured it too, and his figures came out to more. His father, a man who believed in white folks and didn't want to hurt their feelings, was shocked.

"Don't do that, son," he said. "The white folks will never like that."

But Esau waited around until everybody else had gotten their money and then went over to the man.

"You know," he said, "there's something wrong with my cotton, according to what you paid me. And my money didn't come to what it should come to for the amount of cotton I had."

The man checked, and sure enough, he had made a mistake.

Esau said to his father: "Now, Daddy, you see I don't know how long they were doing this, and I don't know how long this man was doing this. This is my first year to start farming. But my price was wrong. And I don't know how many other persons' was wrong, but I didn't say it, because I was afraid that everybody would say the same thing and then he would blame me for it. But can't you see it's good to do your own figuring?"

It was the beginning of Esau Jenkins' conviction about the importance of education.

When he shifted to truck farming he bought a truck to haul vegetables into Charleston. Driving around town, he noticed that most of the stores were run by Greeks. He figured the thing to do was to learn Greek. So he studied it for a couple of years and his business increased by leaps and bounds. Greeks in Charleston, South Carolina, aren't accustomed to Negroes who speak Greek, but they liked it.

Education again.

By 1948 he was operating a bus line from the Island to Charleston. He'd been thinking a lot about conditions on the Island and had come to the conclusion that nothing would get done about changing things until they could get people registered to vote. So he made his bus into a peripatetic classroom, where he taught people to read the part of the Constitution that had to be read for voter registration.

" One of these mornings," he reported later, " while I was teaching the group to read the Constitution, a woman by the name of Alice said to me, ' Mr. Jenkins, I would like very much to become a registered citizen, but I cannot read this Constitution because I did not get but just so far in school, and I can't pronounce these words. But if you are willing to help me, I will show you that I would be one that would be willing to vote in every election.' So I decided to pay more attention to her, and I helped her at more times than I do the regular times when we have school in the bus, to get her prepared to register.

" So when the time came quite a few of us went down to the Board to register, and those with a little formal education went in first. And Alice went in with a few behind. And someone made a mistake in pronouncing a word. Although Alice could not have read it if it were pointed out to her, she started to coach somebody who could read, and the registrar said, ' No coaching in here.' So when it got to her, and the registrar gave her this part you have to read to pass, she read it so fast that the registrar said, ' Well, you can read very well.' "

Alice had memorized the whole damn thing. That's education too.

It was Septima Clark, the number one catch in Ab Sloan's raid on the school, who persuaded Esau to go to Highlander. Septima had begun her teaching career in 1916 on Johns Island where, as an eighteen-year-old high school graduate, she had found herself in charge of 132 Negro pupils of all ages at the princely salary of thirty dollars a month. Not far away a white teacher with the same credential was teaching three white children for eighty-five dollars a month. But Septima, not, as we have seen, one to be easily discouraged, stuck it out and learned to love the Island and its people.

One of her stories about that year just has to be told. It concerns burial practices on the Island, which consisted of stuffing the deceased into a pinto box (a coffin with one square and one pointed end), sometimes breaking his legs to make him fit, and getting him underground after a wake whose length depended on how hot the weather was. This particular loved one was an old man so bent over that in his last years he had walked with his body almost parallel to the ground from the hips up. It was not a condition that made him a comfortable fit in a pinto box. After wrestling with the problem for some hours they decided to strap him down and nail the ends of the strap to the coffin, in which bonds they bore him to the church and placed the half-opened casket in front of the pulpit.

Maybe they used a weak strap or hadn't nailed it down properly. Or maybe the old man was just stubborn. At any rate, just as the minister was finishing his sermon, the strap broke and the dead man sat up in his coffin. A general exodus took place through the church's only door, in the rear, with the minister, who had to come all the way from the pulpit, a dead last. Several hundred yards down the road, as he sprinted by the congregation and the deacons and elders, he was heard to say something that sounded suspiciously like cursing. Hauled up before church authorities a few days later, he was formally accused of taking the name of the Lord in vain and asked if he wished to make a statement.

As Septima reports it in her autobiography, *Echo in My Soul:* " Breth'n," he replied, his eyeballs rolling, " I sho' does want to make a statement. I wa'n't cussin', no, suh. All I said when I went by you all was jes' this: 'Damn a church what don't have but one do '! "

The Island was not greatly changed forty years later when Esau Jenkins began conducting his literacy classes on the bus. You could now drive over a bridge to Charleston instead of taking an interminable trip by boat, but poverty, ignorance, and superstition were still rampant, and the schools were the same kind of one or two room shacks Septima had taught in 1916. There was no Negro high school. Now a teacher on the mainland, highly respected in her profession, a key person in the local NAACP, and a former student and sometime field worker for Highlander, Septima Clark became interested in Esau Jenkins' work on Johns Island and finally persuaded him to go to Highlander.

It was a new world for him, as Highlander was for everyone who came there for the first time, and he soaked it all up in his usual way. At the end of the week, when the time came for the students to describe the immediate problem in their communities, Esau said that his problem was adult education; could Highlander help establish a center on Johns Island where people could be trained to the point where they could register to vote — and beyond?

Highlander could. It loaned $1500 without interest to buy an abandoned schoolhouse and put up the expenses for the teacher, Bernice Robinson, a Charleston beautician and seamstress who was later to become a Highlander staff member and the first victim of Ab Sloan's raid. The school flourished, and on his next visit to Highlander, the following year, Esau asked for help for Wadmalaw and Edisto, islands to the south who had heard about his school. He got it, and in 1960 Wadmalaw registered more voters than in all the previous history of the Island and on Edisto Negro voters outnumbered the whites.

Esau is not a man to take it easy. In 1954 he ran for election to the school board, not in the expectation he could win, since Johns Island then had only 200 registered Negro voters, but to demonstrate that a Negro could run for public office and not get killed. He polled 192 of the 200 potential Negro votes (what happened to the other eight?) and came in third in a field of four. The first Negro voter who went into the booth realized Esau had made his point. " Man," he said when he came out, " Esau Jenkins' name is on that voting machine. You better get down there and vote."

Fifty new voters were registered in 1955; by 1958 the count was more than four hundred. A lot of things happened as a result. Predictably, Esau was offered a bribe to lay off; equally predictably, he refused. Johns Island got its high school, a consolidated grammar school, and school buses to boot. Previously Negro children had walked eight to ten miles a day to arrive at an unheated school where they waited for the teacher, who lived eighteen miles away in Charleston, to open up. After the children were deployed into the woods behind the school to collect firewood, the potbellied stove was lighted and classes would begin.

Perhaps their greatest victory was over a local judge, a man who had a well-earned reputation for always finding Negroes wrong. Once when Esau was riding from Charleston to the Island in a friend's truck, a white man rammed them from the rear. In court the magistrate found the Negro guilty. Some years later, however, after the Citizenship Schools had produced a massive Negro registration, he

Sea Island Progressive Club, Johns Island, South Carolina. PHOTO
BY BOB GAINER.

changed his tune. On his try for election for the third time, the white vote was known to be split almost evenly on his candidacy. He came to Esau for help.

"Well," Esau said, "if you promise to treat Negroes better, if you make them realize they are human beings when they come into court instead of charging them with everything and just assuming they are wrong, if you just give them what belongs to them and let them know they're right if they are right, we'll vote for you."

The judge agreed, the Negroes voted for him, and he won. From that point on he treated the colored people who came into his court like relatives. Which of course they were. All us humans are relatives, though few of us seem able to realize it.

The Progressive Club, which Esau had founded — Progressive because the word meant "look upward, do something better" — had become a political force. And out of it, and the Citizenship Schools, grew Highlander's program of citizenship education, to be ably directed by Septima Clark and later to be transferred to Martin Luther King's organization, the Southern Conference for Christian Leadership (SCLC). Both Myles and Zilphia Horton visited Johns Island and spent the night, to the consternation of most black or white liberal Charlestonians. Primarily as the result of the courage and imagination of one man and one institution, Esau Jenkins and Highlander Folk School, Johns Island had become a focal point for Negro education in the South.

"Everyone is jubilant for Highlander Folk School," Esau reported. "They have helped them see the light. Along with registration, they have taught a good many of them how to sign checks, fill out money orders, how to crochet, how to sew, how to fill out blanks for their drivers' licenses. I think it's been a great success."

*Adult evening classes at the Citizenship School on Johns Island,
South Carolina.* PHOTO BY IDA BERMAN.

Other things were happening on Johns Island too. They were singing. Lord, how they were singing!

The Freedom Movement, which was soon to erupt full-blown, is the singingest movement in American history. Even the labor movement of the thirties, to whose singing Zilphia Horton contributed so impressively, can't hold a candle to it. There is a lot of carry-over, mostly through Zilphia. A number of the songs she collected and edited — the Tennessee State Library and Archives has a 38-page listing of her music collection, which has been microfilmed for research purposes — were revised into freedom songs. Of these, "We Shall Overcome" is of course the most famous.

But singing in the Freedom Movement took a different turn, and Johns Island had something to do with this. Zilphia, in her work with the labor movement, had never neglected folk and popular songs. For example, her *CIO Songbook* contained, besides union songs, tunes ranging from "Down in the Valley" to "Let Me Call You Sweetheart." The point was for people to sing things they felt comfortable with. Such songbooks never contained music, just the words to tunes people already knew.

But in the Negro revolution which has come to be called the Freedom Movement, there was a new source to be tapped, the traditional songs of the Negro people, still carried down through the oral tradition. It may seem contradictory, but this discovery did not come easy. Most young Negroes, those who formed the backbone of the new revolution, were ashamed of this music. To them it represented the church slavery, and the long history of Negro bondage. They wanted no part of it.

After Zilphia's untimely death in 1956 a new folksinger arrived at Highlander, one of the succession which had included Woody Guthrie, Pete Seeger, Frank Hamilton, Jack Elliott, and Cordell Regan. This was Guy Carawan, whom we have already seen interned by Ab Sloan's fuzz, a young Caucasian from California whose native roots were in North Carolina. He had already learned " We Shall Overcome " in Los Angeles from Wally Hille, a former Highlander staff member who was now music director of the First Unitarian Church, so he came prepared. Guy took up Zilphia's mantle and spread it wide. He began to lead singing all over the South, first at the Nashville sit-ins which followed hard on the real explosion of the Freedom Movement, and then all through the area. He also went one step further. He become interested in the authentic negro music that they were singing on Johns Island and a few other places, and put himself in the paradoxical position of being a white man who was teaching young Negroes their own music.

It all came to a head in a " Sing for Freedom " in Atlanta in 1964, jointly sponsored by Highlander, SCLC, and SNCC. The invitation had been aimed directly at civil rights groups. Composed, as usual, by Highlander, it said: " Would you like to know more freedom songs and have better singing at your mass meetings and community gatherings? If so, please carefully choose one or two people in your group who are good at singing and song leading and will be able to learn something at this workshop and festival which they can use to help your organization and local movement."

The Highlander style. Help people to do it themselves.

The Sing-In was an enormous success. On the old campus of Gammon Theological Seminary, a Negro institution, the group was composed mainly of Southerners, colored and white, but with a sizable infiltration of topical singers from the North, most of whom had no previous experience at the heart of things in the South. Tom Paxton, a very talented

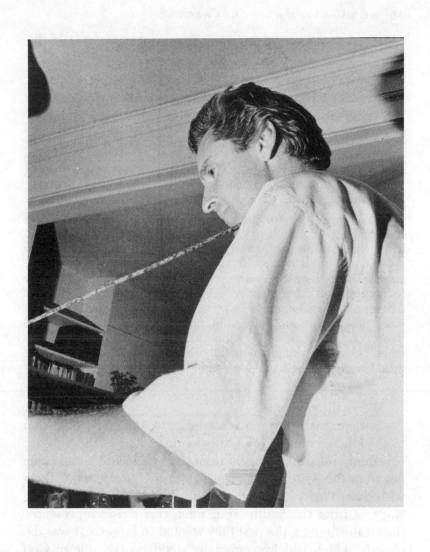

Guy Carawan performing at Highlander Center, August, 1967.
PHOTO BY JOSEPH CARROLL.

Northern composer and singer of protest songs, put it this way:

There is an enormous difference musically between what they're doing and what we're doing, and I wouldn't — I don't think there is any reason to say which is more effective. But I was tremendously moved by the music we heard down there, and the thing that knocked me out was that all those songs were what I call action songs. Songs to be sung in the thick of it with no need for guitars or microphones, or any of it because with the first bar by one man they all know the song.

The songs are structurally set for mass singing which of course is not true at all of our songs, with the possible exception being when people join in a chorus. What we write are essentially musical editorials where, if you agree with me, you sing the chorus. But there the entire song, sometimes with only a few words changed from verse to verse, is sung right in the face of the cops and mobs and they're fantastic. Songs to be sung in jails. They are much more utilitarian songs than ours are. And there is no comparison as to their value to the civil rights movement. Our songs might hopefully line up a little support and a little bread, but their songs are right in the fight.

We shall overcome.

Not curiously, but most interestingly, the major objection to the kind of music Guy Carawan promoted at the Sing for Freedom and which singers from the Sea Island sung, came not from the writers and singers from the North, who, along with Tom Paxton, wanted to learn, but from radical young Negroes from the South. For them this music represented the establishment, the past they wanted to forget. It was the church, which had immemorially stood on the side of God and the White Man.

As one woman said: " I came here to sing and hear freedom songs. I can hear the old songs any time back home.

What do people back home want with it? Why should I bring it back?"

There were three good answers.

One was from Amanda Bowens, a ninety-pound girl from Americus, Georgia, who had spent two months in jail as the result of civil rights demonstrations. "I'm tired of going to church," she said, "and listening to teen-agers giggle and laugh when the old songs are sung. I want to know that my parents were working for fifteen cents a day. What these songs are is what most of this means."

Reverend Young, a Negro minister who was a member of the planning committee, summarized it: "We all know you can't trust a Negro on the negotiating committee who doesn't like his people's music. We learned that in Birmingham! "

But Len Chandler, a Negro musician from New York with a strong background in classical music, summed it all up. "I went through this scene, man," he said. "I was ashamed of Grandmother's music. I went to school to get a degree, in Akron, and things were all put in a nice little box, a package of the Western world's music. But there was nothing in that box about my music. Why, even the spirituals were fitted out to a white audience to sound nice and polite — you know the bit — Marion Anderson. . . . It wasn't until this white professor took me to his house to listen to some tapes that I started to know what my music was about. It took a white man to teach me about my own music. Why this music (Bessie Jones') is great, and the boys on the radios and the TV's have stopped you from hearing it — but this is it, man, this is the stuff."

A great statement, including the remark about Marion Anderson. When she sang Brahms' "Alto Rhapsody" she was one of the greatest contraltos, but when she sang her own peoples' music she condescended. It's the same mistake

Zilphia Horton made at first — the classically trained musician's distrust of folk music. But Zilphia had Myles Horton to teach her. Marion didn't. I don't mean Myles taught Zilphia music. He can't sing his way out of a phone booth and I doubt he can play a juice harp. His sole active contribution to freedom songs was to add a one line (repeated) chorus to "We Shall Overcome": "And the truth will make us free." But he knew the score, and he knew *what* music was important in helping people to find unity and their own identity. That's what Len Chandler was listening to in Atlanta.

A small personal story may illuminate the whole point, which is a fundamental one. When I began to write this book after a long visit with Myles in Knoxville, the trip on which my wife and I first began to sense hate in Alabama, I holed up in an improbable town in Texas named Del Rio. The River, El Rio Grande del Norte — the Great River of the North — it was once called, but that got to be too long a handle for Texans in ten gallon hats, was next door. Del Rio, whose original name was San Felipe del Rio, had also subsided into an abbreviation. But it remains instructional that the Rio Grande is the great river of the North for Mexicans. The South is a pretty big country, and it faces north.

When I'd written about half the book, Myles came down to visit us and correct my infrequent indiscretions. It was Easter weekend, and Sunday we went across the River to Cuidad Acuña to celebrate. We heard a band concert in the Plaza and then drifted to the bar of one of the town's better-known restaurants. There were a couple of Mexican mariachi guitar players there, and they were good. Unlike most *turista,* I didn't just listen: I sang with them. I'm the poor man's Joan Baez. We got going pretty good. But I wanted to do a little more. I wanted to play with them.

Myles and *Zilphia* *Horton* square-dancing. PHOTO BY EMIL
WILLIMETZ.

But I didn't have any instrument. Myles volunteered, being preoccupied with tequila daisies at the time and well back into the saber-tooth era, education-wise, to contribute funds to purchase a harmonica. I accepted, as is my wont. I did even better. He gave me ten dollars, and I purchased *El Centenario*, the cheapest good harmonica you can buy on this continent, and didn't give him back the change. I will admit I bought a couple of rounds for the three of us and gave the mariachi players two bucks. They wanted three but I refused on the grounds that one of those ought to be mine. For this reason.

We got a pretty good combo going. Their English was nonexistent and my Spanish is negligible, but we didn't need words. We just played together, and pretty soon I found I was the leader and began to point, as you do, to who was going to play the solo. Both these guys were terrific on the guitar and I figured the fellow who was playing the accompaniment in their standard routine was a lot better than he had a chance to show, and the first time he had the lead he proved it. He was an Indian, as all native Mexicans began by being, and he gave me a big smile and just turned it on. He was great. Later on, when I was playing the lead in " San Antonio Rose," he gave me a number of *Olé's* which I discounted as signs of his appreciation of his solos. We never exchanged a word except smiles.

This is the way Highlander has always worked with music. People can communicate through this medium when they can't in other ways. But they communicate only through music that is familiar to them — the Mexicans and I had a common core of Latin American and Southwestern American music — and developing an identity with people's own heritage is what Highlander has always tried to do. We didn't try to play anything we all didn't know. That's the basic assumption.

But this was after the revolution, which began very quietly. On February first, 1960, four Negro students walked into a ten cent store in Greensboro, North Carolina, a town you can be excused for never having heard of, and ordered coffee. They were refused service, as was customary in Greensboro, but they did not, as was also customary, leave. They just sat. And waited. And thus began the wave of student sit-ins which transformed protests like Rosa Parks's and Martin Luther King's into a genuine mass movement.

Highlander had a large hand here too. Those four Negro boys didn't walk into the dime store by accident. Young people were in rebellion against older organizations like the NAACP, whose approach was and continues to be legalistic, though they've been trying hard these days to catch up with the kids. A new generation of leaders was developing, with the boys who set up the sit-in at Greensboro making the first overt move, and a large proportion of them were former Highlander students.

The Movement spread like wildfire, an expression which is no cliché if you're a Californian. A few weeks later students were also sitting-in in Nashville, and Guy Carawan was going over to lead them in singing. He even found his wife there, an unexpected bonanza which he deserves. Nobody took the sit-ins very seriously, right then, but the kids were on the march.

Nobody, that is, except Highlander. At a workshop on Social Needs and Social Resources at Highlander on March 18–20, 1960, six weeks after the original sit-in in Greensboro, Myles Horton made the following statement:

" I would like to predict," he said, " that the present sit-ins

Institute for Minority Groups, Fitzgerald, Georgia. A typical Highlander outpost.

mark a new phase of democratic action in America. The efforts of the Negro college students have already become recognized by the Negro community leaders in Nashville and other Southern cities. Already college young people, who a month ago had no opportunity to act as responsible adults, now have grown in stature and self-respect in the eyes of the students and the Negro and white community at large. On the other hand some white adults, including city and educational officials, are acting with immaturity. The men are being divided from the boys."

It all developed out of this — the march on Selma, the massive demonstrations in Albany, the development of new organizations like SNCC which symbolized young Negro rebellion, the full-fledged participation of white actionists in the Negro Movement. And along with it went the steady organizational work Highlander had begun before, the development of the citizenship schools which, under Septima Clark's able direction, blossomed until Highlander, under attack from that courageous fighter for democracy, little old measly old Ab Sloan, passed this benefit along to SCLC.

But the fruits were there. Highlander, about to lose all its possessions, under indictment by the Great State of Tennessee, somehow didn't falter. It moved on to the new Center in Knoxville, and from there our final story begins.

CHAPTER SIX

Conclusion

Another era in Highlander's history had begun. The school still remained deeply committed to the Freedom Movement: with leadership training, citizenship schools, and music, it continued to give guidance and support. Myles Horton participated in demonstrations like the march on Selma and in many workshops and conferences all through the area. Other Highlander staff members did the same, and more than one of them, including Myles, got roughed up for their pains. But nevertheless a new focus was developing. It's important that we pause here and examine the reasons.

Highlander's main emphasis has always been on a very simple thing. It isn't just civil rights. It isn't just labor education. It isn't just community organization. It's democracy. It's the necessity for people to sit down together, regardless of race, creed, etcetera, and talk about their common problems. And try to do something about them. The arena changes. The goal never does.

By the 1960's, the Freedom Movement was established. It had its own leadership and its own momentum. Some of that momentum was going in directions at another compass point from Highlander's. SNCC, many of whose leaders had

A Klan parading by Highlander Center. PHOTO BY CAROL BROWNE.

come, and continued to come, to Highlander's leadership training courses, became the focal point for young Negro militants. And it was moving steadily in the direction of Negro nationalism, of Black Power. This was predictable. Myles and I have talked about it often, and recognized that it was inevitable. We both just hoped the Movement would survive it. But nevertheless you still have to leave it up to the people who are doing things.

There has been an enormous furor in the press about SNCC's attitude, and, more recently, about the activities of smaller groups, now frequently local, like the Black Students' Union at San Francisco State College, to choose one small example. Stokely Carmichael, the late chairman of SNCC, has been under attack for his avowedly racist policies. His speaking out in "unfriendly" countries has made him even more unpopular, and as I write on this December morning in 1967, the Justice Department is considering whether it will be politically expedient to jail him after his return to America. So goes democracy in America in this Anno Domini. It is well to remember what most Americans have forgotten, that passports were originally designed to protect, not restrict, citizens. Although a recent Supreme Court decision has partly reaffirmed this in theory, the court left enough loopholes so that the right of Americans to travel in areas the government does not approve of is likely to continue to be restricted.

It's true that a lot of Carmichael's statements haven't made much sense. Black racism is no better than white racism, as we have noted before and as Martin Luther King has said very eloquently. But there are two differences. Once is that black racism is even more foolish. Negroes are and will remain a minority group in this country. Just from a practical point of view, Highlander's approach is the only one that stands a chance of working for them. The other difference is that Negro racism is a great deal more understandable. You can't oppress people for centuries and not expect that their first real whiff of freedom will go to their heads. Especially when militancy is called for, as it is, Black Power is the logical and inevitable step. In the long haul, the fact that it is self-defeating is the important thing; in the short one, where we are now, the important thing is that it was predestined to happen.

It is useful to remember two things. One is that Stokely Carmichael, along with Martin Luther King, was on the firing line in Canton, Mississippi, where the local cops, during the march on Jackson, reverted to type and threw massive doses of tear gas into the crowd, beat marchers with shotgun butts, and kicked canisters of gas into the faces of people they'd knocked down. If you need an explanation of why Black Power had to happen, you've got it right there.

The other thing is something Myles said to a group in Atlanta not long ago. "You guys don't know enough," he said. "You've got to learn more." He didn't get much response, but he planted the idea. After that you can only hope. Right now the kids are too busy being activists, and with reason, to realize that there are things to learn from the past. If they don't find it out in the long run we're all in trouble. But Uncle Toms have been talking about the past for a long time, and right now the kids have had their fill of it. It's a lot like the ready suspicion of the old Negro music.

I speak as an old radical, a fact which may have faintly emerged before. I distrust all liberals, who are always more talk than do. I have more respect for the John Birch Society, much as I hate their guts, than I do for Americans for Democratic Action. At least you always know where the former stand. ADA-type liberals, a generic term, always sail with the wind. Witness the fact that they were the first ones to propose Dwight David Eisenhower for president — on the Democratic ticket. They didn't have any idea what he stood for or what the quality of his mind, if I may strain a phrase, was: they just thought he could win. That is precisely the right way to lose any basic struggle.

Consider Canton again for a moment. In Madison County, according to a U.S. Civil Rights Commission report, the following happened in two years: five Negroes were wounded by gunshot, the local civil rights headquarters was bombed twice, three other Negro buildings and four churches were burned, and several other Negroes and civil rights workers were assaulted. In only two cases were the persons responsible for this violence arrested and prosecuted. And in both instances, the defendants pleaded no contest and received the minimal fines. Sheriff Jack Cauthen, in charge of keeping law and order by such procedures as those described above, was characterized as revealing hostility to civil rights activities which evidently affected his conduct in office.

Put this in the context we have previously discussed, of a world where most offenses against Negroes are not recorded, and you have the idea. It's no wonder that Stokely Carmichael, speaking from the courthouse steps in nearby Philadelphia (where three civil rights workers had been murdered two years before) at a demonstration where Negroes were allowed to gather provided no one stepped on the grass, said this, pointing to a collection of jeering whites: " Here you see America at its truest form — a sick society. It's up to us to take care of it and we are going to do it in our own way."

The presence of Stokely Carmichael and Martin Luther King, Jr., on the same courthouse steps gives us a confrontation of the basic oppositions in the Movement — SCLC, with

King as the charismatic leader, and SNCC, which is dedicated to the proposition that leadership is of itself a bad
thing. There will be clashes and modifications between these
two wings, but it doesn't really matter. The important fact
is that they have both shown the capacity for coexistence in
a common struggle.

Can you fault Carmichael? Or his successor, Rap Brown?
Not for now.

But in the long run the process of mutual education, the
Highlander way, must continue. The Negro must join in the
process of educating people like Governor Johnson of Mississippi, who is a "racial moderate." In Mississippi parlance
this means that he doesn't say "I hate Niggers" more than
ten times a day. Commenting on Sheriff Jack Cauthen's pres-
ervation of law and order in Canton, where unarmed demonstrators, including women and children, were savagely attacked by police, the Governor had this to say: "The police
acted only after they were surrounded by marchers. The
police action was the humane thing to do, and deterred the
violence. Actually, there wasn't anyone hurt. I don't think
no good can come from this march." (Los Angeles *Times*,
June 25, 1966)

Ignoring the Governor's execrable grammar, a kindness
he doesn't deserve, there are a couple of things worth noting.
The police had been collecting riot equipment for hours before the demonstrators arrived. As the *Times* reports, "reporters and law enforcement officers knew of these plans
hours before the attack on the demonstrators. At least four
hours before the tear gas attack, Sheriff Jack C. Cauthen's
deputies were carrying riot weapons and the sheriff indicated to newsmen that trouble was anticipated. He warned
newsmen that his duties were to enforce the law. 'Please

don't get in our way, because if you do, we're gonna move you.' Several photographers filming the police action Thursday were clubbed by officers."

Since what Sheriff Cauthen was enforcing was the law, no further demonstration of the reasons for the Negro's feelings about Southern justice is necessary. All that the demonstrators wanted to do was to set up tents in the yard of a Negro school, a proposal which Cauthen, in his nonexistent wisdom, had decided was not permissible. The only violence was that which was perpetrated by the police, who were ready and willing to start it. The bravery of the fuzz in meeting an unarmed group, including women and children, with such necessary weapons as riot guns and tear gas, staggers the imagination. It was justice, all right, that the sheriff was enforcing. Justice, Madison County style, as far as the majority of the population — Negroes — was concerned.

So now we come to the real hard nut of the immediate question: what happens with Black Power? It is now a question for Negro leadership, since Highlander, in its characteristic fashion, once an operation has become self-sustaining, has now turned its basic attention, while still continuing full support of the Movement, to another area which is unorganized and needs its organizing skill.

The question of Black Power is not, newspapers, magazines, and public opinion polls to the contrary, a simple one. But there are a few simple facts that need to be considered. White public reaction against Negro violence ignores one of these — the fact that Negroes have lived in an atmosphere of violence against *them* since we forced their arrival on this continent. If they do not now turn the other cheek, they feel, and I agree, that it's about time. It is a fact of our national psyche that we grasp at simplicities which are wrong. One of these is that it is hot weather that causes Negro rebellion.

The ramifications of this view, which has been seriously promulgated all across the country, are fascinating, including just a little thing like air conditioning, but I'll stick to a more basic observation. It isn't the hot summers. It is, for the Negro, the last hot hundred and fifty years.

And there are other things. How do you distinguish between violence and self-defense? The Deacons in Mississippi raised this point and Martin Luther King was pondering it at the time of his assassination. When the Black Panthers invaded the statehouse in Sacramento, the Reagan heartland, now bullet-proofed, they were making the same gesture. You can't expect people to be continuously pushed around and then repeat God Bless America. Not even out of tune.

So what's to be done? There aren't any political organizations to join. The socialists have thrown in the sponge; the communists are working dutifully for their own establishment, located thousands of miles away but looking more like America every day, and vice versa; all the civil rights groups are focused on necessary but more limited goals. What do you do about trying to achieve democracy?

What about the whites in that mob who were jeering Stokely Carmichael and Martin Luther King? What do you do about them? They are ignorant, prejudiced, and impoverished. They are expressing their discontent with their lot in the only way they can feel superiority — the color of their skins. It doesn't do any good to say this is irrational, as liberals do, or to go in the same if opposite direction, as SNCC and Carmichael are now doing, by plugging for black racism. The Southern poor white is there, he's going to be there, and he represents the majority of the population of the South. What he needs is education, and a way to find a security which is not based on prejudice.

There's not any organization to help. The old left is impotent and the new left isn't interested. But that doesn't make the problem get up and go away. Things like the Federal Anti-Poverty Program, which predictably turns into political patronage systems, won't do anything either. What's needed is to create a new organization where people can sit down together, realize that they have common problems, and do something about them.

That means Highlander. And we're back to community organization again. But on a different scale.

The programs in Summerfield and Grundy County failed because the area was not large enough to be politically important. The problem now is how to organize a whole region. The question is how to convince a farmer in Arkansas and an unemployed miner in West Virginia that they have the same problems. It isn't enough to tell them they're both poor. They know that. But what do they have in common that they can organize around, as people did in all the incidents we have previously examined?

Highlander has begun to hold workshops on this, and people are now out working on this Project. Such developments as the Marrowbone Folk School in Poor Bottom, Kentucky, are an evidence that progress is being made. Does this mean that we have found a way to revitalize democracy in the South and in America?

I don't have the answer to that. Nobody else does either. But if it isn't found, God help us all. We'll continue to be presented with a series of meaningless choices and remain in a bind which only gets worse every year. If anybody can find the answers, it's Highlander.

That's what the Center is presently engaged in.

Let us pray.

Main building, Highlander Center.   PHOTO BY JOSEPH CARROLL.

In the two year interim between first writing this book and publication, a lot has happened. Most of it has proved me a true prophet, but a prophet can feel no honor in his own country when he has witnessed the murder of Martin Luther King and Robert Kennedy and has endured the escalation, conducted under the opposite term, of genocide in Vietnam.

The situation hasn't changed; it has only intensified. The whole notion of integration, or even of Black Power, no longer has any meaning in the ghettoes. What Black Militants want is liberty, the right to run their own show. In view of increasing police armament, from automatic weapons to tanks, the idea of nonviolence is going out the window. Blacks are now fighting back, and for the first time they are getting their share of the kills. I don't see how you can fault them for pleasure in this.

But, as we have observed, this is both good and bad. If Black separation is both necessary and self defeating, what's the answer?

Resurrection City provides a partial answer. Highlander had a tent there, from which Myles Horton tried to organize a coalition of Blacks, Chicanos, and Indians. The attempt was not successful, despite the fact that Tijerina was the most effective leader on the scene. The problem was that Negroes and Blacks, to use a distinction now of great consequence in the ghettoes, dominated the scene. They had little concern for other people of color, and even less for whites. It was in the lower echelons, among the people who did the busywork of the March, that this was particularly apparent. However, despite Abernathy's inept leadership, this is not surprising. Blacks have had few chances to exercise power in America; small wonder they enjoyed it now.

But was this a smart answer?

No.

So let's take a hard look at a prognosis for the future.

Most basic problems have simple answers, and this one is no exception. I did *not* say simple cures. Cures are generally long and arduous, and here again there is no exception. We are in for prolonged violence unless Blacks achieve a significant autonomy in their own communities — a position which whites simply take for granted for themselves. Violence is, tragically, what the white Establishment is ready and eager for, especially the forces of what we call law and order, despite their pious protests against it. Violence erupts when the fuzz moves in, and this will become increasingly true. Increasingly also, black people will be fighting back. Black people are enraged, and justifiably so, that after almost two hundred years of white violence they are now accused of having created it all.

But there is another side to this, one which Resurrection City illustrates. Two alternatives lie ahead: an American police state, toward which we seem to be rapidly heading, or the pluralistic society which the Highlander idea exemplifies. If we are to achieve the latter, blacks must learn to cooperate with whites, browns, yellows, and reds before it is too late.

This is a hard thing to say. Cooperation with whites is the key to this equation, and most whites are even less interested in cooperation than militant blacks are. Secure in their majority position in our society, they ignore the lesson that both history and the blacks should be teaching them, that in refusing to work together with black people they are in the process of destroying themselves.

The trouble is that the same thing is true for blacks. The mythos of the superiority of black pigmentation is just as absurd as the comparable notion about white pigmentation. Only bigots are better because of their color. It is true that the black culture has permitted freer emotional life; the corollary assumption, now rampant in the black community, that only blacks have souls is ridiculous. The crude fact is that militant blacks are acting exactly like whites.

Another basic problem was also illustrated by Resurrection City. What was important there was not black domination, from the rejection of Tijerina to the belated and phony appointment of Chief Black Snake as Chairman of the Council after he had made the scene outside the Supreme Court Building, but the fact that no basic questions were introduced by the leadership of the march. All of Abernathy's demands, none of which were met further than they would have been anyway, involved superficialities. The Poor People's March became a joke, an occasion for commentators to criticize the poor for acting like the poor.

What is imperative is a demand for radical changes in the American power structure. Most black militants and white radicals understand this, although they have not yet learned to work together. The Chicanos do, as Tijerina and Chavez have demonstrated, and the Indians are learning.

White liberals don't understand it at all. The center of the American power bloc, white collar or blue collar, white or black but all middle class in orientation, understands it even less. And there we sit.

This way the signs are all marked Police State.

So what do we do to reintroduce America to the American tradition? I hear lots of people talking about the American tradition, but I see almost no one acting on it. We have had only one revolution in this country. Men died in it, though it has now been whitewashed to look like Tom Sawyer's fence. It didn't look that way to the boys who got shot and buried. Now we need another one. Tom Jefferson said we needed one every generation, but no sage has ever been more misquoted than he, and this eminently practical suggestion is generally conveniently ignored. One option is a political movement such as we have not seen since Eugene Debs. But he ended up in prison for opposing World War I, his movement shattered, and I see no new leaders who could succeed half as well as Debs failed.

The other answer is power, black, white, brown, yellow, and red, plus all our intermixtures. As my favorite black militant in Los Angeles, a beautiful woman with natural hair and green eyes says, "I been integrated in the most fundamental way." But we have to do it all together, something Margaret and her compatriots are not yet ready to do. It is up to all of us who reject the establishment to hang together. Or most assuredly we shall all hang separately.